Murder Most Vile
Volume 37

18 Truly Shocking
Murder Cases

Robert Keller

Please Leave Your Review of This Book at
http://bit.ly/kellerbooks

ISBN: 9798758107775

© 2021 by Robert Keller

robertkellerauthor.com

Table of Contents

No Pain, No Gain

The storyline reads like the plot of a poorly conceived crime novel. And indeed, this tale of bumbling criminals and incompetent cops was made into a Hollywood blockbuster, albeit one that presented the horror of the grisly case as dark comedy. But there was nothing funny about the "Sun Gym murders." This was savagery at its most extreme, murder at its most horrific. It happened in mid-90s Miami.

Jorge Delgado had met multi-millionaire businessman Marc Schiller through his wife, an employee at one of Schiller's companies. The men had quickly become friends, with Delgado a regular guest at Schiller's South Miami mansion. Jorge and Marc had even started a business together, investing in real estate.

Then, in 1994, Jorge Delgado struck up another friendship, with a man named Daniel Lugo, a personal trainer at the Sun Gym in Miami Lakes. He started to bring Lugo to Schiller's house, something that quickly began to irritate Schiller. He didn't like Lugo, didn't like his shifty eyes or the way that he appraised everything in the house as though planning a burglary. Eventually, Schiller asked Delgado to stop bringing Lugo around. Then he issued an ultimatum. Either Delgado stopped hanging out with Lugo or their business dealings were over. Delgado refused and Schiller subsequently withdrew from the real estate business, leaving his partner deep in the hole.

This falling out between business associates would have far-reaching consequences. When Delgado complained to Lugo that Schiller had "cheated" him, Lugo suggested doing something to get even. He might just have been talking tough (something he was inclined to do) but Delgado immediately picked up on the idea. Soon the pair had concocted a plan, a plan that involved kidnapping Schiller and forcing him to sign over his assets, which they'd split between them.

This would require planning, of course. Lugo was going to need help in snatching Schiller. Fortunately, he had that covered. He had plenty of musclebound buddies hanging out at the gym. Then there was the issue of having the deed documents notarized. That would require a notary public and Lugo knew just the man for the job. John Mese was the owner of Sun Gym. He was also a certified accountant.

And so, the plan was set in motion. On November 15, 1994, Lugo, along with associates Noel Doorbal and Carl Weekes, snatched Schiller from the parking lot of Schlotzsky's Deli, a business Schiller owned near Miami International Airport. Schiller was bundled into a van and taken to a warehouse that Delgado had rented for that purpose. There, he was tied to a chair and beaten, then shocked with a Taser. The gang demanded that he sign the documents that were put in front of him, documents that would transfer ownership of his house and other assets. But Schiller was tougher than they thought. Badly beaten, burned with cigarettes, soaked in his own urine when they refused to let him go to the bathroom, he steadfastly refused. It was only when they threatened to bring his wife and children to the warehouse and subject them to the same treatment that he eventually relented.

Lugo now had the deeds to Schiller's house, the code to his safe, the passwords to his bank accounts. But before he could go about harvesting his ill-gotten gains, he needed to get Mrs. Schiller and the kids out of the way. He therefore told Schiller to call his wife and instruct her to leave the country immediately, taking the children with her. Mrs. Schiller, a Colombian national, asked few questions before complying.

Now Lugo had a clear run at Schiller's assets. With the documents notarized by John Mese, he moved into Schiller's mansion and started living the life, splurging his victim's money on cars, clothes, jewelry, and partying. He told Schiller's neighbors that he had bought the property at a "knock-down price" and hinted that he was a retired CIA agent. He said that he now made a living providing security for celebrities. In the meantime, Marc Schiller was still tied up in the warehouse, where he'd now been held for three weeks. The issue of what to do with him was becoming urgent.

Lugo would later claim that it was never his intention to kill Schiller, that he had always planned on letting him go, once he had control over his assets. It is difficult to see how that could have worked. In any case, by mid-December, the gang had decided that Schiller would have to die. On December 15, 1994, Schiller was forced to consume enough alcohol to make him pass out. He was then brought to a remote road in the gang's van with one of the gang members following in Schiller's vehicle. This was driven into a pole before Schiller was placed in the front seat. The car was then doused with gasoline and set alight. The idea was to make it look as though an inebriated Schiller had been involved in a car accident.

But Schiller would prove his resilience once again. As the gang was about to leave, he staggered from the burning vehicle. Lugo then floored the van, hitting Schiller at high speed and driving him under the wheels. He even threw the vehicle into reverse and drove over the unfortunate man again. The gang then left, confident that their victim was dead. He wasn't. Schiller was found soon after and rushed to Jackson Memorial Hospital. There, doctors performed emergency surgery to remove his ruptured spleen. When Schiller regained consciousness, he told hospital staff of his ordeal and asked them to call the police. Two detectives were sent to take his statement but if Schiller was expecting some kind of police response, he was to be sorely mistaken. Rather than taking his story seriously, the officers accused him of lying to avoid a DUI charge.

Marc Schiller had been kidnapped, tortured, robbed of everything he owned. His abductors had forced him to send his family away and had tried to burn him alive. And yet, the Miami police were refusing to do anything about it. Desperate, Schiller contacted private investigator Ed Du Bois, a former Miami-Dade detective. Du Bois listened to Schiller's story and asked him to put everything in writing. Then he started looking into Schiller's claims and discovered to his amazement that the fantastical story was true.

In early February 1995, Du Bois set up a meeting with Sun Gym owner John Mese and confronted him with the documents he'd notarized. Mese admitted that both parties had not been present at the time of signing, an irregularity that could land him in hot water. He denied knowing anything about kidnapping and torture but agreed to set up a meeting between Du Bois and the main players, Lugo and Delgado. When that meeting took place, on February 13, Lugo failed to show. Delgado, meanwhile, was insisting that the whole thing had been a legitimate business deal. Asked about Schiller's accusations of kidnapping and torture, Delgado responded with a terse "no comment." He was clearly rattled though. The meeting ended without a resolution although Delgado promised to meet with Du Bois again, once he'd "spoken to his partners."

That meeting would be held a week later, with Delgado putting an offer on the table. He would return Schiller's money and property. In return, Schiller was to sign a legal document, pledging never to tell anyone what had happened to him, especially not the police. Du Bois said that he would put it to his client.

Shiller, quite unsurprisingly, was none too keen on the terms. Of course, he wanted his money back but the idea that his torturers would get off scot-free was irksome to him. However, after talking with his lawyer and learning that such an agreement would not be legally enforceable, that it would, in fact, amount to a confession, he agreed.

Over the next few days, drafts of the document passed back and forth between the parties. In the meanwhile, the Sun Gym gang vacated Schiller's property, taking everything of value with them. This was in direct contradiction to the agreement, and it was also becoming clear to Du Bois that Delgado was not going to comply with his side of the bargain. It was time to call his bluff. In late February 1995, Du Bois contacted the Metro-Dade police. He expected an emphatic response to allegations of kidnapping, attempted murder, and wholesale fraud. What he got instead were allegations that his client was making the whole thing up.

It is easy to see why the Sun Gym gang might have been emboldened by this lack of police response. Their grand plan had been a horribly botched job but to them, it must have seemed like pure genius. They had, after all, gotten away with it. In any case, they decided to do another one. Their target, this time, was a Hungarian immigrant named Frank Griga, who had made his fortune running a phone sex business. On May 25, 1995, Griga was invited to a meeting at Noel Doorbal's house, ostensibly to discuss an investment opportunity. The plan was to subdue him, to drag him off to the warehouse and torture him into signing over his assets. A carbon copy, in other words, of the Schiller abduction. Unfortunately for the gang, Griga complicated things by bringing his girlfriend, Krisztina Furton, along.

Lugo and Doorbal could have abandoned their plan at this point, or at least delayed it. Instead, they plowed right ahead. Doorbal tried to subdue Griga who fought back, triggering a vicious fistfight. Furton then started screaming at which point Lugo grabbed her and injected her with Rompun, a horse tranquilizer. Meanwhile, Doorbal had gained the upper hand and had Griga in a headlock. He kept applying pressure, maintaining his grip until Griga passed out. Doorbal thought that he had rendered Griga unconscious. In fact, he had cut off his victim's oxygen long enough to kill him. Lugo, too, had been overzealous in his attempt to silence Krisztina Furton. He'd overdosed her with the tranquilizer, causing her breath to become erratic. Still he pressed her for the access codes to the couple's luxury Intracoastal property, jotting down her barely coherent words with a pencil. Soon she stopped talking. Then she stopped breathing.

The Sun Gym gang had launched their latest escapade with dreams of cash and property. All they had to show for it was two corpses that they needed to dispose of. The bodies were loaded into their van and taken to the warehouse, where Lugo and Doorbal performed the grisly task of dissection, using hatchets and a chainsaw. The body parts were later packed into steel drums which were welded shut and then dumped in a drainage ditch in a remote area of Dade County. Another drum containing the heads, hands, and feet of the victims, was deposited in the Everglades.

On May 27, Lugo flew to the Bahamas, where he tried to access Frank Griga's bank account, using the information he'd gained in Krisztina Furton's dying moments. However, the information proved to be inaccurate, and Lugo returned empty-handed to Miami. His gang had similarly been unable to get inside the couple's home. All that the double homicide had gained them was Griga's Lamborghini, which Lugo foolishly insisted on driving around town, thus drawing attention to himself. It resulted in his arrest on June 3, 1995, a week after the murders. Also taken into custody were Noel Doorbal, John Mese, and another gang member, John Raimondo. Warrants would soon follow for Jorge Delgado, Carl Weekes, and Stevenson Pierre.

Brought to trial in July 1998, Lugo and Doorbal pleaded not guilty but were undone by the testimony of their co-accused, Jorge Delgado, who'd turned state's evidence in exchange for a 13-year prison term. Lugo and Doorbal were both convicted of first-degree murder and sentenced to death. They currently await execution. As for their co-conspirators, John Mese was convicted on extortion and racketeering charges and was sentenced to 30 years imprisonment. He died behind bars in 2004. The other members of the bumbling crew received terms ranging from ten to seven years. All have since been released.

There was one more twist to the case, one that added insult to injury for the unfortunate Marc Schiller. Directly after testifying against his abductors and torturers, Schiller was leaving the courthouse when he was arrested by federal agents. He was accused of Medicare fraud and was subsequently sentenced to 46 months in prison. Released in 2001, Schiller claimed that he was innocent of the charge but had pleaded guilty simply because he had "no more fight left in him."

Chosen by God

Zak Valentine   Cecilia Steyn   Marinda Steyn

Le Roux Steyn   Marcel Steyn   John Barnard

It is a story that beggars belief, the horrific tale of a murderous clan, rampaging through suburbia on an unprecedented killing spree, leaving a trail of mutilated bodies in its wake. But what is truly shocking about this astounding saga is that the perpetrators were not hardened criminals but seemingly ordinary people. One of the key players was a middle-aged, high school English teacher; another was her daughter, a Straight-A student who was just 14 years old when she participated in her first murder; another was a millionaire businessman. And then there was the supposed motive behind the killings. Although later murders would be financially

motivated, the killers began their campaign of terror believing that
they had been chosen by God to do his work.

It started in early 2012, when a woman named Cecilia Steyn
became a member of the Overcomers Through Christ church in
Roodepoort, South Africa. Shortly after joining the congregation,
Steyn confided in the church leader, Ria Grunewald, that she had
recently been involved in Satanism and now feared for her
immortal soul. According to Steyn, she was possessed by demons.
She begged Grunewald to pray for her and Grunewald was only
too happy to do so. Overcomers Through Christ follows a literal
interpretation of the scriptures and believes firmly in demonic
possession. In Cecilia Steyn, they appeared to have a genuine case.
As church members prayed for her deliverance, Cecilia writhed
and thrashed and screamed. On one occasion, she even coughed up
blood.

But that blood spewing incident turned out to be less about some
malicious demon and more about a blood capsule that Cecilia had
swallowed. When Ria Grunewald found out, she confronted Steyn
and accused her of lying and of making a mockery of God's work.
Outraged, Steyn quit the church, taking congregants Zak and
Mikeila Valentine and Marinda Steyn (no relation) with her. They
were soon joined by Marinda's children, 14-year-old Marcel, and
17-year-old Le Roux. Another man, John Barnard was also co-
opted into the group which now went by the name Electus per
Deus (Chosen by God).

Schisms within Christian sects are hardly unusual. Indeed, they
hark back to the very foundations of the religion. But Electus per

Deus was no ordinary offshoot. Its motivation was less about the tenets of the faith and more about vengeance. Cecilia was still fuming over being ousted. She wanted payback. Before long she was telling her followers that Overcomers through Christ was a front. They were actually doing the devil's work. According to Steyn, she had heard a senior member of the congregation, Natacha Burger, uttering the "danger prayer," supposedly a Satanic verse that calls for harm to be done to young children. As true servants of Christ, Steyn told her followers, they had a duty to intervene.

On July 2, 2012, members of Electus per Deus entered the parking lot of the Overcomers through Christ Church while a service was in progress and planted several petrol bombs between the cars. Fortunately, they were spotted before they could detonate the devices and fled the scene. Later that month, they started a fire and broke windows at the Lighthouse Christian Centre, a church affiliated with OTC. They also targeted Ria Grunewald with an intimidation campaign. She arrived at the church one day to find a note pinned to the front gate. "Ria," it read, "Who is going to protect you now?" Just days later, Steyn and her followers successfully detonated petrol bombs outside an OTC meeting, destroying four cars. After that, Ria Grunewald went into hiding. She was wise to do so.

On July 26, 2012, Zak and Mikeila Valentine paid a visit to Natacha Burger, the woman Cecilia Steyn had supposedly heard wishing harm on children. Natacha was not home and so the Valentines called on her neighbor and friend, Joy Boonzaier, who was also a member of OTC. Talking their way in, they produced a gun and forced Joy to write a note, asking Natacha to come over to her apartment the minute she got home. This was pinned to Natacha's door and lured her straight into a trap. Both she and her friend were stabbed to death.

Steyn had now struck back at the church that had rejected her. But what she really wanted was to hurt Ria Grunewald. And since Grunewald was now in hiding, she did the next best thing, taking out her wrath on Ria's long-time friend and mentor, Reginald Bendixon. The retired pastor was 71 years old, although he still occasionally gave lectures at OTC. Zak Valentine and Marinda Steyn visited him on August 13, 2012. They were dressed as police officers and claimed to be investigating the Burger/Boonzaier murders. The elderly pastor let them in and ended up being hacked to death with an axe. Marinda Steyn would later describe her first kill as "exciting, an adrenaline rush."

And Marinda would soon have the opportunity to kill again. Mikeila Valentine had been struggling under a burden of guilt over the murders she'd been involved in. She wanted to leave the group and urged her husband to do the same. That left Zak with a decision to make. Who was he going to choose, Mikeila or Electus per Deus? In the end, he chose the latter and that meant that Mikeila had to die. Her guilty conscience was too much of a risk.

On October 4, 2012, Zak Valentine enjoyed breakfast with his wife before leaving for the office. He was barely out of the door when Mikeila began to feel tired, the result of a tranquilizer that Zak had slipped into her coffee. Mikeila went to lie down and was fast asleep when Marinda Steyn entered the house, using a key that Zak had given her. Accompanying Marinda on this mission was her

14-year-old daughter, Marcel. Mikeila Valentine would never wake again. She was stabbed multiple times as she slept, and her skull was caved in with some heavy object. She was just 25 years old on the day that her life was ended.

Over the next three years, the members of Electus per Deus kept a low profile. There had been an investigation into the murders, of course, but they were still unsolved. Zak Valentine had been at work when his wife was killed and thus had a solid alibi. Meanwhile, Ria Grunewald's assertion that her church was under attack by Satanists, barely made it as a footnote into the police dossier. Cecilia Steyn and her gang of psychopaths were off the hook for now. They were also running out of money, having burned through the entirety of Zak Valentine's two-million-rand fortune.

It was John Barnard who came up with a potential solution to their problem. Barnard was employed by a wealthy businessman named Peter Meyer who, according to Barnard, kept up to a million rand in a safe at his home. All they'd have to do was find a way in, threaten Meyer with violence, and force him into giving up the combination. A meeting was thus set up between Zak Valentine and Meyer, ostensibly to discuss a business deal. Valentine was accompanied on this "mission" by Marinda Steyn and her daughter, Marcel. The trio arrived at the Meyer residence on the evening of November 27, 2015, and quickly made their intentions clear. Peter Meyer and his wife were threatened with a gun as Valentine demanded the combination to the safe. Meyer had no problem giving that up, but the strongbox turned out to contain only a few hundred rand. And that spelled doom for the captive couple. Angered by the measly haul, Valentine went to the kitchen and fetched a knife. Peter Meyer was stabbed to death in front of his hysterical wife. Then Valentine turned the blade on Joan and extinguished her screams.

The next money-making scheme that was contrived by the group, came from the sick mind of Valentine himself. He came up with an insurance scam in which he'd take out a policy, name Cecilia Steyn as his sole beneficiary, and then stage his own death. The idea was to fake a road accident in which his luxury Mercedes Benz would catch fire and be totally destroyed, supposedly with Valentine inside. For this to work, Valentine would need someone to take his place in the wreck, but he already had that covered. He'd recently befriended a young man who lived in Cecilia Steyn's apartment building.

Jarod Jackson made a paltry living as a street vendor and so he was immediately interested when Valentine asked him to accompany him to the Free State province for a high-paying job. The pair set off on this road trip on December 16, 2015. Unbeknownst to Jackson, they were being followed by another car, carrying John Barnard, Marinda Steyn, and her son Le Roux. At some point during the journey, Valentine offered Jackson a soft drink which he accepted. A short while later, he began to feel drowsy. Within just a few miles, he'd passed out.

Like Mikeila Valentine before him, Jarod Jackson had been drugged. Now the gang got quickly to work. They pulled the Mercedes SLK into a field, along a remote stretch of the R57 freeway, between the towns of Reitz and Petrus Steyn. There, Valentine strangled his sleeping passenger to death. The gang then doused the vehicle with gasoline and set it alight before driving away from the scene.

It was Marinda Steyn who identified the body in the burned-out Mercedes as Zak Valentine. Given the state of the charred remains, her near-immediate identification should have aroused suspicion. It didn't. A death certificate was issued, declaring Valentine deceased and opening the way for a 3.57-million-rand payout. Unfortunately for the gang, the insurance company red-flagged the claim, meaning that there would be an inquiry. It would lead, eventually, to the arrest of Zak Valentine, who had been hiding out at a church compound in Krugersdorp, a small town southwest of Johannesburg. Now he was looking at a charge of insurance fraud and quite possibly of murder.

With Valentine out of the picture, the members of Electus per Deus lowered their sights somewhat. They now embarked on a series of "appointment murders," targeting various professionals, killing them for a pittance. The first to die in this way was 57-year-old Glen McGregor, a tax consultant. On January 27, 2016, Marinda Steyn, Le Roux Steyn, and John Barnard arrived at McGregor's home in Randfontein, supposedly for a consultation. Instead, they threatened the man with a gun and forced him to transfer 6000-rand into Marinda Steyn's account. McGregor was then executed, shot to death in his own living room.

The next victim, Anthony Scolefield, was also a tax consultant. He was lured to Cecilia Steyn's apartment in Krugersdorp, supposedly to provide tax advice. There he was forced at gunpoint to hand over his wallet and provide the PINs for his various accounts.

Marcel Steyn was sent to a nearby ATM to ensure that the numbers Scolfield had given were correct. With that established, the 67-year-old was of no further use to the gang. He was strangled to death. Over the days that followed, the gang drew over 16000-rand from his accounts and also racked up various charges on his credit cards. Anthony Scolefield's body was later found stuffed into the trunk of his car. By then, the gang had already claimed two more victims.

Kevin McAlpine, a 29-year-old insurance broker, was lured to Cecilia's apartment on May 26, 2016, and strangled to death. Just three days later, 52-year-old realtor, Hanlé Lategan, met a similar fate. That brought the death toll to eleven with no sign that Electus per Deus had any intention of slowing down. Fortunately, there was a glaring problem with the gang's M.O. and it was about to bring them down.

As anyone who has ever used an ATM is no doubt aware, these cash points are under heavy surveillance. The killers quite obviously knew this, since Marcel and Le Roux, who usually made the cash withdrawals, always wore a cap or a hoodie and kept their faces averted from the screen. These efforts, however, were insufficient. Within weeks of Hanlé Lategan's murder, Le Roux Steyn was in custody and his sister soon followed.

Eighteen-year-old Marcel hung tough under interrogation. She was clearly her mother's child. But Le Roux proved far more fragile and was soon blurting out the entire blood-drenched story to stunned detectives. Within days, Cecilia Steyn, Zak Valentine, Marinda Steyn, and John Barnard had also been arrested and charged with multiple counts of murder. John Barnard would later strike a deal with prosecutors. It is through his testimony that we are able to unpick the horrendous details of the murder spree.

What was clear from Barnard's evidence (and from other Electus per Deus members) is that Cecilia Steyn was the leader of the group. Steyn did not participate directly in any of the murders, but it was she who called the shots, she who decided who would be targeted, she who decreed who would die. Zak Valentine was the executioner in chief, along with Marinda Steyn, the bookish, gray-haired English teacher.

The others all had roles to play, whether directly or as accomplices. That was reflected in the sentences that were handed down. Eleven life terms for Cecilia Steyn and Marinda Steyn; eight life sentences for Zak Valentine; seven for Marcel Steyn. Le Roux Steyn, who had played a part in seven of the murders, was given 35 years for each, as agreed in his plea bargain. John Barnard had already accepted a term of 20 years in prison, in exchange for his testimony. None of them will be walking free any time soon.

Stop the Clocks

It should have been a case of 'happily ever after' for Peter Harvey and Lorna Smith. The pair had started dating as teenagers, had a daughter together in their twenties, and married ten years later in 1999. But the fairy tale romance would not stand the strains of married life. Within two years, Peter had told Lorna that he'd met someone else. The split was amicable but heartbreaking for Lorna. She and Peter had been together for 20 years, all of her adult life. Desperately lonely, she turned to a friend for solace.

Clifford Mills had been Peter Harvey's best friend, had been best man at his wedding. But the pair had had a falling out since then and Mills had stopped coming around. Lorna hadn't seen him for over a year when she made contact on Facebook and asked if he'd like to meet for coffee. That turned out to be a pleasant diversion, a few hours spent swopping nostalgic stories about the 'old days.' Thereafter, Cliff became a regular visitor at Lorna's home in Croydon, south London. Within six weeks, he'd moved in.

This arrangement did not sit well with Lorna's 13-year-old daughter, Louise. She didn't like Cliff...and with good reason. The hefty, overweight Mills was bossy and overbearing. He didn't work and would spend his days in front of the television, drinking beer and stuffing his face with snacks. Then, when Lorna arrived from work, he'd switch to dictator mode, demanding his dinner and expecting to be waited on hand and foot. He controlled every aspect of Lorna's life, telling her what to wear, what to eat, who she could talk to, where she could go, and for how long. He also controlled her finances, even though he contributed nothing to the household. Louise couldn't understand why her mother put up with it.

Mills also had another odd quirk. He was obsessed with the comedy duo Laurel and Hardy and had developed an alter-ego who he called Stan, after Stan Laurel. Except that Mills' version of 'Stan' wasn't even mildly funny. He was an aggressive, angry individual. When Mills was in a bad mood, he'd warn Lorna and Louise that "Stan is about." The message was clear. They were to leave him alone or face the consequences. The women would spend the rest of the evening on tenterhooks. This, after all, was a man who like to boast of his exploits as a football hooligan, a man who'd once earned his living as a nightclub bouncer. He was not someone you'd want to annoy.

Eventually, after three years of living under these conditions, Louise had had enough. She told her mother that she was moving out and going to live with her father. Lorna was close to her daughter, but she'd been so thoroughly brainwashed by Mills that she made no complaint. Mills, meanwhile, was delighted to have

Louise out of the way. He now had Lorna under his complete control.

But the long-suffering Lorna was also reaching her breaking point by now. In 2006, a year after Louise moved out, she told Mills that she wanted out of the relationship. Given the man's threatening persona, this must have taken some courage. But Mills' response surprised Lorna. He started crying, told her that he couldn't live without her, threatened to kill himself if she left him. A compassionate individual, Lorna was moved by this. She told Mills that he could stay, although not as a lover. From now on, he'd be a boarder in her house.

Mills might not have been too pleased with this arrangement although he agreed to it. To him, nothing much had changed anyway. He'd still be able to keep Lorna under surveillance and on a short leash. As for the rest, it didn't bother him too much. Due to his impotence, it had been a long time since he and Lorna had been intimate.

And so, an uneasy truce descended on the Croydon property, one that was shattered when Mills discovered that Lorna had taken to online dating. That triggered an outburst during which he called her a 'slut' and then resorted to mewling self-pity of the 'how could you do this to me' variety. Lorna was quick to remind him that they were no longer in a relationship but that made little difference to Mills. He would continue moping and sulking around the place for months until he eventually told Lorna that he was moving out and returning to his flat in Brixton. This was undoubtedly a contrived move. In Mills' warped view of reality, he probably imagined Lorna begging him to stay. Instead, she offered to help him pack.

Lorna was free at last, free of emotional manipulation, servitude, and the ever-present threat of physical violence. Now free of Mills' malign influence, she decided that it was time to enter the dating game again. Despite her experiences with Mills, she still believed that Mr. Right was out there for her. After opening a Facebook account, she set about navigating the murky world of online matchups. That was how she met Charlie Manning.

Charlie was everything that Cliff Mills was not – kind, understanding, and caring. He told her that he was a wealthy property developer and that he'd 'treat her like a princess' if they were together. Lorna, vulnerable after two failed relationships, lapped up every word. When Charlie asked about her previous boyfriends, she told him about Cliff and their troubled relationship. To her surprise, Charlie urged her to stay in contact with Cliff, suggesting that he was probably lonely and needed her as a friend. To Lorna, this was indicative of Charlie's compassionate nature. She took him at his word, re-establishing contact with Cliff and even visiting him once a week to clean his apartment.

What Lorna didn't know was that she was being manipulated. There was no Charlie Manning. The man behind the keyboard was none other than Cliff Mills. Perhaps the absence of a profile picture (or of any photographs at all, for that matter) should have been a clue. But Lorna didn't want to hear it, not even when her daughter, Louise, voiced her suspicions about who Charlie Manning really was. She continued corresponding with him for over a year before eventually breaking it off. When she did, it wasn't because she believed that she was being played but rather because she'd found love in the real world.

It happened when a co-worker asked her out. Lorna said yes and agreed to a second date after the first went well. Soon, she and her colleague were an item, much to the delight of her daughter, Louise. She hadn't seen her mother so happy in years. It seemed, at last, that she had found the partner she desired, the love that she deserved.

But not everyone was as pleased with Lorna's newfound happiness. Charlie Manning, a.k.a. Cliff Mills, was never going to take the news well. When Lorna messaged him and told him that she'd met someone, he was furious. When she said that she would be ending their online correspondence, he was positively seething. In Mills' warped psyche, Lorna was his. No one else was going to have her. No one.

And so, a truly dreadful plan was set in motion. While Lorna basked in the glow of new love, her ex took to the internet, hunting for a way to salve his bruised ego. The searches he conducted over the next few days are indicative of what he had in mind – 'how to kill with a knife,' 'how to kill a human being,' 'samurai sword for sale.' Throughout mid-January and into February 2011, he planned this, alone in his dimly lit flat, crouched over his computer with murder in his heart. Eventually, he acted, placing a call to Lorna and asking her to come to his apartment to help him with some paperwork. Ever the compassionate soul, Lorna said yes. The

meeting, in any case, would serve a secondary purpose. She
needed to let Cliff know that she was moving on with her life.

On the afternoon of February 3, 2011, Lorna Smith arrived at the
Brixton apartment of her ex-boyfriend. She would never leave. At
some point during the visit, Mills crept up behind her and struck
her on the back of the head with a pick handle. His intention was
to render Lorna unconscious, but she was only stunned. She
collapsed to the floor but immediately tried to regain her footing
and defend herself, suffering defensive wounds to her arms and
wrist as he continued the onslaught. In truth, Lorna never stood a
chance. She was a petite woman, her attacker a hulking, beefy man
with a history of violence. The unfortunate woman was pinned to
the floor as Mills drew a knife and inflicted seven savage wounds
to her torso. Then, as Lorna's screams died down, he pulled the
blade across her throat, cutting deep, severing vital blood vessels.

Lorna Smith was dead, cut down at the age of 45 for no other
reason than exerting her right to make her own choices in life. To
the man who had slain her, this was vindication. Such was the
nature of the beast that he felt he'd acted within his rights. He
could not, however, bear to look at Lorna's face, locked in the
pained grimace of violent death. He pulled a plastic bag over her
head to hide that accusatory look. Then he packed a bag, raided his
victim's purse for cash, and left his apartment for good. He paused
just long enough to turn on the stereo and cue a song, playing it on
a loop – Stop the Clocks by Oasis.

Mills would spend the rest of that day riding tubes and buses
before settling down eventually at a Soho bar, where he steadily

drank himself through the money he'd stolen from his victim. He showed up the following morning at St. Thomas' Hospital, where he told a startled receptionist, "Stan has killed Lorna. You need to call the police. I love her, Stan hates her. He killed her."

This would be the constant refrain in the run-up to Clifford Mills' trial. He admitted that it was he who had stabbed Lorna but denied responsibility for her death. He admitted manslaughter but denied murder. It was all the fault of Stan, his murderous alter-ego, Stan who 'lives in my head.' He was still singing this tune when he was rolled into court in a wheelchair in January 2012, doing his best to look frail and confused and vulnerable. It was a quite pathetic display.

Unfortunately for Mills, he had bought into a popular (but false) perception of multiple personality disorder. In a genuine case, the various personalities are not aware of each other, and the host is not cognizant of any of them. By blaming 'Stan' for the murder, by acknowledging that he was aware of Stan's presence, he was effectively defeating his own argument.

In the end, it took the jury just 90 minutes to convict. The date, fittingly, was February 3, 2012, the first anniversary of Lorna's death. Clifford Mills was sentenced to life in prison. He must serve a minimum of 21 years before he can apply for parole. By then, he will be in his seventies.

The Talented Mr. Rycroft

Growing up on the tough streets of Salford, near Manchester, England, Glenn Rycroft had a plan. He was going to escape his humble beginnings and carve out a good life for himself. He knew that he had what it takes to succeed. He was reasonably intelligent, forward-thinking, and personable. In fact, that was his strongest quality. People liked Glenn. He got along with everyone. It was a personality trait that would serve him particularly well in his first job, as a flight attendant for British Airways.

But that job, much as he liked it, was never going to get Glen to where he wanted to be, living the high life, driving a flashy car, traveling the world as a first-class passenger rather than a glorified waitron. And so, Glenn Rycroft came up with a scheme. In September of 2000, he started approaching friends and family about an investment opportunity. He told them that BA had launched an investment vehicle called the "British Airways Investment Bond." This was a capital guaranteed scheme that was projected to return between 20% and 23% in just twelve to eighteen months. The scheme was only open to BA employees, but

Rycroft was prepared to do them all a big favor. He'd invest any funds that they gave him under his own name. He'd then pay them the proceeds once the investment reached its expiration.

With returns like this, a guarantee of capital, and the backing of one of the world's foremost corporations, it is not surprising that there were many takers. Rycroft's brother-in-law, Paul Shaw, put in £26,000; a business associate, Glanville Gough, invested £10,000; Rycroft's uncle, John Rowlands, contributed £5,000. Others invested even more. The mother of an old school friend gave £43,000. Her sister wrote a check for £55,000, her entire life savings.

What these trusting investors didn't realize was that they'd never see their money again. There was no "British Airways Investment Bond." It was all a scam. Their money wasn't being invested; it was being used to finance a lavish lifestyle for Glenn Rycroft. He rented a luxury apartment, leased a top-of-the-range German sedan, bought a small business, took holidays in Florida and the Bahamas and Australia, bringing several friends with him. Rycroft had landed exactly where he wanted to be, and he'd achieved his goal just a couple of years into his working life.

But one thing that Rycroft hadn't considered was an exit strategy. His lies would not hold up forever. Sooner or later, his investors would want to see a return on their money, the fabulous return that he'd promised them. With no way to make good on those promises, he'd be exposed as a fraud. He'd probably be arrested and might well end up in prison. At the very least, he will have humiliated himself in front of friends and family. The clock was ticking.

And so, Rycroft dreamed up another scam, one that would discourage anyone from pressing him for money. In November 2000, he asked for a period of unpaid leave from British Airways, saying that his mother had been diagnosed with terminal cancer. He then told a different lie to his family and friends. To them, he claimed that an aggressive cancerous tumor had been found on his brain and that he was on extended sick leave from BA so that he could receive treatment. Even so, he wasn't expected to survive and had less than twelve months to live.

Rycroft played this horribly callous falsehood to the hilt. He typed up a letter on stolen stationery from a local hospital, supposedly confirming his diagnosis; he shaved off his hair to emulate the effects of chemotherapy; he lost weight; he even carried around a supply of fake blood capsules, which he'd use to "cough up blood" to gain sympathy. Now, when his investors asked for their money back, Rycroft could shame them for being insensitive and claim that the stress they were putting on him was worsening his condition.

But Rycroft's latest scam wasn't just employed passively to ward off irate investors. He used it to raise new funds by claiming that he had to travel to Australia, to undergo expensive medical treatment that was only available in that country. Even those who were already in the hole to Rycroft were taken in by this sob story. Family and friends rallied around to raise over £20,000 for his bogus treatment. Then Rycroft decided to cast the net wider. He began organizing fund-raising events, set up collections at local clubs, ran various raffles which offered flight tickets, supposedly donated by British Airways, as a prize.

We don't know for certain how much money was raised via these dubious means. But it was enough to finance yet another round of elaborate holidays. Favorite locations like the Bahamas and Florida were revisited and Rycroft also spent time at a five-star golfing resort in Portugal. This, despite the fact that he didn't play the sport. He then toured the United States before traveling to Australia with two friends in tow. These individuals were just two more victims of Rycroft's maneuverings. They believed that they were there to support a friend with a life-threatening illness. In truth, they were being shifted around like pawns in Rycroft's sick game. He'd leave them alone for days at a time, saying that he had to go to some secret location for treatment. Then he'd return, looking weak and frail, to lap up the sympathy they lavished on him.

These machinations were undoubtedly satisfying to Rycroft, perhaps even more satisfying than the money he was scamming. But the game that he was playing was about to unravel and it would do so in a classic example of poetic justice. Rycroft had played his con too well. So heart-rending was his performance as a terminal cancer sufferer that his local community rallied behind him, taking up the cause of fundraising. In October 2001, a benefit concert was organized by his supporters, with various performers donating their services and all receipts going towards Rycroft's cancer treatment. The con that Rycroft had so carefully constructed was about to go public, generating attention that he didn't want.

The compere for the fundraising evening was a woman named Debbie Henley who, coincidentally, worked for British Airways, Rycroft's former employer. After hearing that the airline had previously donated free flights as prizes for Rycroft's raffle, Debbie suggested that they get the company involved in the charity evening. However, Rycroft was adamant that he didn't want BA involved and even insisted that Debbie stand down as compere. This struck Debbie as an odd response. All she was doing was trying to maximize the amount of money raised through the charity evening. Why the hostility?

The answer to that question was soon forthcoming. As Debbie delved a little deeper, she began to uncover several inconsistencies in Rycroft's cancer story. The most jarring was something that Rycroft had shared with a number of people. He'd told them that his former company had a jet permanently on standby, ready to fly him anywhere in the world should there be a breakthrough in the treatment for his disease.

This sounded highly unlikely to Debbie and so she decided to query BA about it the next day. It was then that the extent of Glenn Rycroft's lies began to be exposed. The ludicrous "jet on standby" story was quite obviously a lie. But Debbie also found out that Glenn had resigned from the company some months earlier, something he'd been at pains to hide from the local community. Then Debbie learned of the fictitious investment scheme that Rycroft had been running and knew that it was time to report the matter to the authorities. The charity event would go ahead but the money would be donated instead to a local children's hospital.

As for Glenn Rycroft, he'd spend the evening in police custody. He would ultimately be convicted on 25 charges of obtaining money by deception. His various schemes had netted him an estimated £200,000, money that would never be recovered. He would pay for it with a four-year prison sentence, although he was released after serving just half that time.

By 2007, Rycroft was a free man, looking for a new score. A gay man, he started trawling the hookup site Fit Lads, looking for someone to fleece. That was how he met 29-year-old Gareth MacDonald, a married father-of-two whose wife was pregnant with their third child. McDonald had long had questions regarding his sexuality. After hooking up with Rycroft, he abandoned his wife and children to set up home with his lover in Rhewl, North Wales. It is uncertain whether McDonald knew of Rycroft's checkered past. If he did, Rycroft must have convinced him that he'd been judged unfairly. Why else would McDonald have poured money into a travel company which the two men started together?

The rest of the story follows a predictable path. The company's bills went unpaid, and McDonald soon realized that money was being siphoned out of the business and out of his personal bank account. This resulted in an angry confrontation between the men during which McDonald accused Rycroft of being a con artist. Over the days that followed several texts were exchanged between the lovers, with McDonald telling Rycroft that he still loved him but wasn't sure if he could trust him any longer. Rycroft responded that he hoped to win back that trust, beginning with righting a previous wrong. His uncle, John Rowlands, was visiting the UK from Canada. Rycroft wanted to pay back the £5,000 he'd taken from him in the BA investment scam. That would require a road trip to London. Would MacDonald care to accompany him?

McDonald, of course, said yes. Rycroft was nothing if not persuasive. The couple set off on their journey on September 14, 2007. However, Rycroft took a number of wrong turns along the route, and they ended up hopelessly lost and having to overnight at the Travelodge near Heathrow Airport. In the early hours of the following morning, Rycroft left the hotel, driving away in his car. He was back within minutes, returning to his room. Just moments later, he came running into reception, shouting that his friend had been attacked.

That would turn out to be a significant understatement. Gareth MacDonald had not just been attacked, he'd been killed, struck so hard on the head with a fire extinguisher that two semi-circular fractures were left embedded in his skull. Questioned by police, Rycroft initially said that he'd left the room to buy a glucose monitor for his partner, who was diabetic. He had returned to find MacDonald clubbed to death. Later, he would offer another story. He now claimed that MacDonald had hired a male prostitute and that he'd left the room to give them some privacy. The implication was clear. This 'rent boy' was the one who had killed MacDonald. He was the one that the police should be looking for.

However, neither of Rycroft's stories tallied with the evidence. Hotel staff testified that he'd been out of the room for just a couple of minutes. This was at odds with the timeline of his version of events. Then there was the murder weapon, which was covered in his fingerprints. Rycroft claimed that this was because he'd picked up the item earlier in the evening. Even if that were true, how did he explain the blood spatter on his shoes and trousers? Still protesting his innocence, Rycroft was arrested on suspicion of murder.

Over the days that followed, the police would strengthen their case. This murder, it appeared, was not a spur-of-the-moment thing. Rycroft had been thinking about it for some time. His internet search history turned up terms like, 'how to kill someone by injection', 'how to break a neck', 'effect of a blow to the head' and 'fall down stair kills'. There was also a manuscript, apparently the first few chapters of an autobiography that Rycroft was writing. While this did not provide any evidence that was directly incriminating, it did offer an insight into Rycroft's state of mind. In it, he likened himself to Tom Ripley, the character played by Matt Damon in the movie, The Talented Mr. Ripley. Ripley is a young man from a modest background who seeks to improve his lot in life through deception and murder. Much the same could be said of Glenn Rycroft.

Rycroft was ultimately convicted of murder and sentenced to life in prison with a minimum term of 25 years. The inmates who share a cellblock with him had better keep an eye on their commissary money.

Yesterday's News

Augusta Nack

It started on the glorious Saturday afternoon of June 26, 1897, when two boys decided to take a dip in New York's East River, close to the Brooklyn Navy Yard. The cool water was a blessed relief from the mugginess of the day but the boys knew they shouldn't linger too long. This was a busy shipping lane. They were just about to turn for shore when one of them spotted a bundle, wrapped in red and gold oilcloth, bobbing with the swell. Thinking that it might contain something valuable, the boys got a grip on the object and towed it to shore. It was heavy, waterlogged. Eagerly, they dragged it onto the bank and started undoing the cord that secured it. Then the package fell open and the boys recoiled in horror. It contained a headless torso with the arms attached.

The next morning, some 150 blocks away, Julius Meyer and his two sons were picking blueberries in the barrens along the Harlem River when they spotted a parcel hidden in some bushes. The package was wrapped in a garish red cloth, decorated with a gold diamond pattern. It was bound with a cord which Julius quickly unravelled. Inside was the lower abdomen and upper legs of a man. The lower legs would be fished from the East River later that same day. They, too, were wrapped in the distinctive red and gold cloth.

News of the horrific find spread like wildfire across the city. But the police were quick to quell the accompanying panic. At first, they wrote it off as a prank by medical students. Then, after the coroner confirmed that this was not some ill-advised lark, they reluctantly opened a docket. They were less than enthusiastic about pursuing the case. The force was stressed and overextended, ill-equipped to adequately police a burgeoning metropolis of 3.4 million souls. The murder of some unknown individual, probably of the lower or criminal classes, did not figure high on their agenda.

But it did feature on the agendas of the city's rival tabloids, William Randolph Hearst's New York Journal and Joseph Pulitzer's New York World. These papers were a fairly recent addition to the media scene and offered a different type of journalism to the staid New York Times. Their stories were raw and brazen, focused on sensational (and sensationalized) fodder. Body parts afloat in the East River was just their speed.

And so, the *Journal* and the *World* threw money and manpower at the story. They were better financed than the police and their reporters were as adept as any NYPD detective at sniffing out clues. Chief among these was George Arnold, a seasoned newshound with a reputation for thinking out of the box. While others were scurrying around trying to uncover the identity of the mystery corpse, Arnold turned his attention to the cloth that held the remains. He soon learned that the fabric was manufactured by the H.F. Buchanan Company. Next, he obtained a list of stockists in the New York area and found that this specific batch had been shipped to a merchant in Astoria. Questioned by Arnold, the seller reported that the line was not popular. He'd only sold one swath of the cloth in recent weeks. It had been purchased by a Mrs. Augusta Nack of Manhattan.

Mrs. Nack turned out to be a heavy-set German woman who was qualified as a midwife but now made her living running a boarding house at 439 Ninth Avenue in Hell's Kitchen. According to rumor, she supplemented her income by performing illegal abortions. Arnold also learned, through local gossip, that Nack was currently involved in a love triangle with two fellow Germans, William Guldensuppe, a powerfully built masseur, and Martin Thorn, a handsome but hotheaded barber. Guldensuppe had been Mrs. Nack's live-in love for the past two years, ever since he'd supplanted her husband. But it seemed that Thorn had recently muscled in on the action and had been spending time with Mrs. Nack whenever Guldensuppe wasn't around. The two men had come to blows over the affections of the portly temptress and Thorn had come off the worse for it. He'd suffered a couple of vicious beatings. Now, it appeared, both of the men were missing.

Having followed the evidence this far, Arnold decided that it was time to call in the NYPD. The payoff for his work would be a heads up on any information coming out of the police inquiries. The first order of business was to identify the dismembered remains in the morgue. Who better to provide that information than Augusta Nack. She was taken into custody and brought to the station.

But if the police thought that Mrs. Nack might buckle under interrogation they were misguided. Nack denied that she'd been intimate with either Thorn or Guldensuppe and indignantly told detectives that she did not know where either man was. Flustered after hours of trying to break her down, detectives resorted to desperate measures. They carried in the severed legs recovered from the river and slammed them down on the table.

"Do you know those?" a detective demanded.

"I do not," Mrs. Nack replied, without batting an eye.

It was clear that the police were going to have to try something else. They visited a Turkish bath that Guldensuppe had frequented and questioned its patrons. One of the men they spoke to agreed to view the grisly body parts and quickly declared that he recognized them. His identification was based on two things. William Guldensuppe had a scar on his finger which the man recognized. He'd also had a tattoo on his chest, a tattoo that was now missing. A square of flesh had been carved from the corpse's torso, apparently in an attempt to impede identification.

So now the corpse had a name. But the police still had very little evidence that would point them in the direction of a suspect. Knowing where the murder had occurred would help but that might be anywhere in the five boroughs. They had no way of knowing. It would take an unexpected tip to point them in the right direction. A workman reported that he'd spotted a substantial puddle outside a cottage in Queens. He found this unusual because it hadn't rained recently. Also, the water was a strange color. It had a pinkish tinge to it.

Officers soon descended on the property and located the landlord who said that he'd recently rented it to a Mr. and Mrs. Braun. His tenants had yet to move in, he said, but he had noticed an unusual spike in water usage, which suggested that they might have spent time at the house. In fact, they'd used up 40,000 gallons of water over just a couple of days!

And if that water had been used to wash away trace evidence of a murder, it had been put to good use. The place had been scrubbed clean. Try as they might, the detectives could not find a single drop of blood. Then one of their number, Detective JJ O'Connell, had an idea. O'Connell had worked as a plumber before joining the police force and he now put his former training to use, disassembling the sink traps and pipes. There, caught in the bends, was a foul-smelling red paste that could only be one thing. They'd found their crime scene.

The case was slowly building, and the detectives now set about identifying the mysterious Mr. and Mrs. Braun. The landlord of the cottage was shown a picture of Augusta Nack and immediately nodded his head in recognition. "That's her," he said. He was then asked to describe "Mr. Braun" and the description he provided sounded a lot like Martin Thorn. But where was Thorn? Rumor had it that he'd boarded a ship bound for Europe. If that was the case, it was unlikely that he'd ever be caught.

But Thorn hadn't fled. He was in hiding in the city but had been in touch with fellow barber, John Gotha, who now contacted the police. According to Gotha, Thorn had confessed the murder to him. He'd said that it had all been Augusta Nack's idea. She had wanted to end her affair with Guldensuppe but was afraid that he would never let her go. She'd therefore asked Thorn to kill him. Thorn had been willing to go along with it because Guldensuppe had previously beaten and humiliated him.

On the day of the murder, Nack had invited Guldensuppe to the Woodside property, ostensibly to talk about a business opportunity. Thorn had been hiding in a closet. He'd stepped out as Guldensuppe passed him and shot his rival in the back of the head with a revolver. That had not killed Guldensuppe but had critically injured him. According to Thorn's telling of events, he'd cut off his rival's head with a straight razor, "while he was still breathing."

Now Thorn and Nack got to work, discarding the evidence of murder. First, they dragged Guldensuppe into the bathroom. Then they lifted him into the tub and started dissecting him, using a saw, a razor, and several knives. The body parts were all wrapped in cloth, all except the head, which was encased in cement. The pair then hauled these bundles to the nearest landing and boarded a ferry, carrying their heavy load with them. They tossed the head overboard first and were happy to see it sink immediately beneath the waves.

However, the next bundle, containing the chest and arms did not sink and neither did the third, containing their victim's legs. Horrified, the pair kept the final bundle with them, later hiding it in woodland close to the Harlem River. Afraid now that they'd be discovered, they decided to split up, with Thorn going into hiding. Their plan was to flee the country and to reunite later, back in their native Germany. However, they would never get the chance. Following a tip-off, police swooped on a rooming house on 25th Street, Manhattan, and took Thorn into custody. In his possession, detectives found a small valise stuffed with newspaper clippings about the case. Like everyone else in New York, he'd been following the story.

The matter finally came to trial in November 1897, at the Queens County Courthouse. To accommodate the expected flood of spectators, admission was by ticket only and ticket requests were oversubscribed many hundreds of times. The court also had to put in extra benches for the 72 reporters who had flooded in from around the country. Ten extra telegraph lines were installed, and a room was even set aside to house carrier pigeons, who would fly from the courtroom to deliver dispatches to newspaper offices across the river.

And the reportage was certainly dramatic. Once united in their silence, the lovers turned on each other once the proceedings got underway. Nack insisted that the whole thing was Thorn's idea and that she'd only gone along because she was afraid of him. Thorn told a different story. He said that Guldensuppe was already dead when he arrived at the cottage, killed by Mrs. Nack. He admitted that he'd helped dispose of the body but denied murder. According to him, Nack had wanted Guldensuppe dead because he was about to report her illegal abortion operation to the police. Adding to the drama was the adversarial stance of the two defense attorneys. They openly traded insults and almost came to blows on the courthouse steps.

In the end, it was Martin Thorn's injudicious confession to his friend John Gotha that proved the difference. Both of the conspirators were found guilty, but Thorn got the death penalty and Nack got just 15 years in prison. He died in the electric chair at Sing Sing on August 1, 1898. She would spend just under a decade at Auburn Prison before her release in 1907.

Nack was initially inundated with interview requests on her return to New York. But she demanded payment for her time and the papers soon lost interest. Ten years had passed since the infamous murder and the public had long since moved on. The story of Augusta Nack and the "Woodside Horror" was yesterday's news.

Terror in Tenerife

The island of Tenerife is a tourist haven, a jewel in the crown of Spain's Canary Islands archipelago. Famous for its majestic volcanic peak, its sandy white beaches, its nightlife, and its year-round great weather, it is a magnet for holidaymakers, attracting over six million visitors a year. It is particularly popular with the Brits, who come in their droves.

Jennifer Mills-Westley had been a frequent visitor over the years and had fallen in love with the island. So much so, that when she retired from her job with the Norfolk County Council, she decided to move there permanently. Part of her retirement funding was used to purchase two apartments in a whitewashed, hilltop development in Port Royale. Jennifer occupied one of these herself and generated income from the other by renting it out to tourists. It was a good life, even though the 60-year-old grandmother had recently voiced concerns to her daughter over the rising crime levels on the island.

Part of the problem was the influx of vagrants. Drawn by the mild
climate and the year-round presence of tourists to badger or to
steal from, these drifters had flocked in from across Europe. Most,
but not all, were harmless. Take Deyan Valentinov Deyanov, for
example. The 28-year-old Bulgarian national was from the town of
Ruse. His father was a former communist party official who had
struck it rich in the post-Soviet scramble for cut-price state assets.

That should have set Deyanov up for life had he not displayed such
a propensity for criminal behavior. He was a drug addict and a
compulsive gambler, who frequently stole from his family to fund
his habits. Eventually, his father had had enough, cutting him off
and ejecting him from the familial home. Deyanov then hit the
road, traveling across Europe and spending time in Cyprus,
Scotland, and the north of England. He ended up, eventually, in the
small Welsh town of Bodelwyddan. There, his bizarre behavior
landed him in the psychiatric unit at Glan Clwyd hospital, where he
would remain for the next three months. He was discharged in
October 2010, despite showing no noticeable signs of
improvement. Sometime thereafter, he crossed back to mainland
Europe and made his way to Spain. He arrived in Tenerife in early
2011.

Deyanov set up home in a partially built house close to Los
Cristianos beach. This had been intended as a luxury residence,
but the owner seemed to have abandoned the project, allowing
squatters to move in. The place was littered with garbage and
defaced with graffiti. It stank of urine and unwashed bodies.
Within these unsavory conditions, Deyanov had laid claim to a
corner which consisted of a filthy mattress, a couple of cardboard
boxes filled with his belongings, and a shrine made out of breeze

blocks, featuring a picture of Christ and a charred copy of the Bible. This was a fitting centerpiece since Deyanov was by now in the grip of a severe case of religious mania. During his short time in Los Cristianos, he'd become a familiar, if unwelcome, figure. He'd walk the streets shouting threats and dogma, claiming that he was a messenger of God, sent to strike down the unbelievers. Most people gave the wild-eyed crazy a wide berth. Few, however, considered him to be dangerous.

But Dyanov's anti-social behavior was escalating, spilling over into more worrying territory. In February 2011, he launched an entirely unprovoked attack on a security guard, in front of hundreds of stunned onlookers along the Los Cristianos seafront. That offense saw him arrested and sent to the psychiatric unit at the Hospital de la Candelaria. He would spend several days under observation although charges were ultimately dropped. He'd barely been released when he was in trouble again, this time for harassing women outside a nightclub in nearby Playa de las Américas. Then there was an incident on May 12, 2011, when he walked into a store and asked the startled clerk for a 'big knife' so that he could 'kill someone'. The police were then called but Dyanov was long gone before they arrived. He was left roaming the streets, carrying his knife and hunting for a victim. Just one day later, he'd find her.

Friday, May 13, 2011, was a mild day in Tenerife, with the temperature hovering in the mid-60s and partly cloudy conditions overhead. There was also an occasional spattering of rain but that did not deflect Jennifer Mills-Westley from her usual routine. She had grocery shopping to do in Los Cristianos.

The high street was already heaving with pedestrian traffic by the time Jennifer got there. Despite the throng, she quickly became aware of a man who appeared to be following her. The man was strongly built, unkempt, dressed in dirty jeans, his face scowling out from beneath a hoodie. Was she being paranoid? Jennifer didn't think so. The man was clearly tracking her, making every turn she made, close enough so that he'd be able to reach her in just three long strides. Despite the crowds around her, Jennifer began to fear for her safety.

In fact, Jennifer was so frightened that she walked into a social security office and asked for help. The staff there noticed just how terrified she was. Tears were glistening in her eyes, as she spoke. They reassured her that all would be okay. In the meantime, one of the clerks kept a watch on the man through a window. He was loitering on the sidewalk, muttering to himself as he walked in a tight circle, his hands plunged deep into the pockets of his hoodie. Then he seemed to think better of hanging around and lurched off, blending quickly into the crowd.

Jennifer would remain in the social security office for five more minutes. Then the staff told her that her stalker was gone and that it was safe for her to leave. She was thankful to be away. She had just one more stop to make, at a supermarket called Shung, in the busy Avenida Juan Carlos shopping mall. Once that was done, she could head on home, lock her door, and put the stressful events of the morning behind her.

But Jennifer would not make it home that day. She'd only just entered the supermarket with the man, the same hulking stranger who'd been following her earlier, walked up behind her. Jennifer was oblivious to his presence as he reached into the pocket of his hoodie and drew a large butcher's knife. Without saying a word, he plunged it into Jennifer's back.

Jennifer screamed, spun around, put up her hands to protect herself. Meanwhile, pandemonium was breaking out around her as screaming shoppers scrambled for cover. That did nothing to distract the attacker from his purpose. The knife was raised, plunged into the petite woman before him, raised again. Thrust after thrust was landed, fourteen in all, before the knifeman delivered the killing blow, drawing the knife across Jennifer's throat. Now the killer dropped to his knees beside his felled victim and started sawing at her neck. It was quite clear what he intended.

Removing a person's head from their body is no easy task. With the dull blade that Dyanov had at his disposal, it took nearly five minutes to hack through the spinal column. But the killer was determined and eventually, he had the result he wanted. He walked from the supermarket holding Jennifer Mills-Westley's severed head by the hair. "This is my treasure!" he shouted at the horrified crowd, which had fallen back into a jittery semi-circle around him. "God is on earth!" He then tossed the head aside and it was at that moment that a brave security guard lunged in and tackled him to the ground.

Deyanov was taken to a police station in Playa de las Americas and held there overnight. He was later charged with murder and then moved to the psychiatric unit of a local hospital. Since the entire attack had been caught on the store's surveillance cameras and since the bloody murder weapon had been found in his possession, there was no point in denying responsibility. Deyanov made no attempt to do that. Instead, he claimed that he had no recollection of committing the murder and did not recognize himself on the video footage. He was a paranoid schizophrenic, he said, and therefore bore no responsibility.

This was exactly the narrative that Deyanov's defense team brought into his trial. "My client is not guilty of any crime," his lawyer informed the jury. "It would be a travesty of justice to hold him responsible."

Brazen though this defense was, it appeared to be a valid legal argument. The accused was, after all, a man who had been sectioned under the Mental Health Acts of two separate countries. But a quirk of Spanish law meant that Deyanov would not escape justice. He had launched an unprovoked attack on his victim, giving her no opportunity to defend herself. Under the prevailing statute, that rendered his mental condition moot. He was guilty of murder and the nine-person jury declared him thus. Asked if he had anything to say after the verdict was given, Deyanov declared: "I am the second reincarnation of Jesus Christ and I will bring the fire of the Holy Spirit to bear against this court."

Threats of divine retribution notwithstanding, Deyan Deyanov was sentenced to 20 years in prison, to be served at a secure psychiatric facility. That means that he will be eligible for release while still in his forties, a frightening thought.

Blowback

The box, with its bright red Marshall Field's gift wrap, had been sitting on Marcus Toney's coffee table for almost a week. He'd been afraid to open it, afraid of what it might contain. "It's a VCR," his friend, Alphonso Butler, assured him.

"I know that," Marcus replied. He had already peeled back a section of the wrapping to reveal the print on the cardboard box underneath. It wasn't so much the Sony VCR he was worried about; it was what might be loaded on the machine. Marcus was sure that it was a sex tape of his wife, Lisa. The couple was estranged, and Marcus had moved out of their condo in Dolton, Illinois, and was living at one of the rental properties he'd acquired over the years. During their separation, he'd become convinced that Lisa was seeing someone else.

And those suspicions had escalated over the past week. Ever since he'd found the mysterious package sitting on his front porch, he'd been receiving messages on his answering machine pressing him to open it. "Why don't you take a look at what I sent you?" the taunting male voice urged. "Why don't you look inside?" Thus far, Marcus had resisted.

The mysterious box, the taunting phone calls, and his estrangement from his wife, were not the only problems that Marcus Toney was dealing with at that time. Recently, he'd become the victim of identity theft. A cautious man by nature, Marcus kept a tight rein on his finances. Just lately though, he'd been inundated with calls from banks and collection agencies. Someone had taken out several credit cards in his name and was running up massive bills on them. This unknown person had also leased two luxury vehicles – a Lexus and a Mercedes Benz – for which Marcus was now being harassed over non-payment. All in all, he was in the hole for $200,000. He'd taken the matter to his lawyer and currently had a private investigator working the case. He had his suspicions about who was responsible. He was certain that Lisa and her new lover were behind it.

But back to the box, sitting there on the table, a taunting reminder of everything that was wrong in Marcus Toney's life right now. "Come on, man," his friend Alphonso urged. "Just open it already. At least then you'll know. One way or the other, you'll know where you stand."

Perhaps it was that which spurred Marcus into action, the need to know. He leaned forward and started ripping at the gift wrap. Then he ran a letter opener along the strip of duct tape that held down the flap. That done, he got a hold on one end of the flap and peeled it back. That was when the bomb exploded.

Alphonso Butler, standing slightly to the side of the detonation point, found himself lifted from his feet, thrown across the room, sent smashing through the window. He ended up on the Muskegon Avenue sidewalk, temporarily deafened, badly hurt, but still breathing. Marcus Toney was not so lucky. He'd taken the full force of the blast, an explosion that ripped off his left arm, severed his feet at the ankle, and propelled a large chunk of shrapnel into his chest. The autopsy would later reveal that this jagged piece of metal caused fatal lacerations to Marcus's heart. The only consolation was that he went quickly.

So how did Marcus Toney, husband, small-scale property investor, and day-time janitor at City Colleges of Chicago, end up the target of a bomb plot? To answer that question, we need to introduce the third player in this drama, a Haitian national named Sienky Lallemand.

Sienky Lallemand was a character straight out of Hollywood central casting. In 2000, when our story takes place, he was 31 years old, a glib, handsome man who had turned the art of seduction into a profitable profession. But Lallemand's interest in women wasn't romantic or even lustful. He was a con artist, whose sole purpose was "the game," as he called it. His targets were vulnerable females working in positions where they had access to useful information – bank employees, insurance company employees, women who worked for state or federal agencies. His M.O. was to charm these women, bed them, and then pump them for information.

Lallemand's criminal career had started a decade earlier, when he was a married man, unemployed, and living in Calumet City, Illinois. Close to his apartment was a forest, where he often jogged in the morning. It did not take long before he realized that the area was a cruising spot for gay men looking for sex. Ever the opportunist, he soon had an idea on how to profit from this intelligence. One October day in 1991, while his wife was at work, he lured a man back to his apartment for sex. Unbeknownst to this man, the entire encounter was captured on film. He soon found himself the target of blackmail, with Lallemand demanding $16,000 to stop him going public with the tape. Unfortunately for Lallemand, his target was not intimidated. He went to the FBI and Lallemand found himself charged with extortion. He was ultimately sentenced to 18 months in federal prison. It was behind bars that his criminal education really began.

Lallemand's cellmate was a man named Anthony Gomillion, a con artist who specialized in identity theft. Gomillion took a shine to his young cohort and soon began teaching him everything he knew – how to set up a fake identity, how to trick people into providing personal information, how to fleece the financial institutions, how to siphon off money to overseas bank accounts. By the time Sienky walked free in 1994, he had plenty of technical expertise to go with his undoubted charm.

The next move for Lallemand was to Indianapolis, where he set up a dummy corporation, Leopold Financial, and started running scams. His accomplice in all this was a transgender woman named Sherri Payne (real name Frances J. Burkhart), a sometime lover of Lallemand. Their partnership was initially successful, but it would soon attract the attention of law enforcement. Within a year,

Lallemand was behind bars again. He remained there until his release in late 1996. Just over a year later, he met Lisa Toney.

Lisa was, at this time, a happily married woman. Or at least so it seemed. In truth, she was bored with her marriage, bored with Marcus, looking for some excitement. Enter Sienky Lallemand. Lallemand was living at his parents' home in Dolton, right across the street from the Toneys. While pushing his niece on her tricycle one day, he spotted Lisa. Forty-something and somewhat pudgy, she wasn't really his type.

But Lallemand had a predator's instinct. He instinctively identified Lisa as a target and moved in on her. The fact that she was a mid-level manager of telecommunications giant, Ameritech, would have made her an attractive mark to him. In no time at all, he had seduced her, and the pair became lovers. Then he followed a familiar path. He started pressuring Lisa into stealing documents from her husband, documents that he was able to parlay into a fake identity and an unprecedented spending spree. He even set up a mailbox and diverted Marcus's correspondence to it. Marcus wasn't even aware that he was being scammed until he started receiving calls demanding payment for charges he hadn't incurred.

Sienky Lallemand was an incorrigible thief and con man. But if one thing could be said in his favor, it was that he was not a violent man. Lisa Toney, on the other hand, was not above committing murder to get her way. What she wanted was a life with her handsome young lover and to get that her current husband had to go. Lallemand was initially against the idea of killing Marcus, until Lisa reminded him that Marcus had a lawyer and a private eye on the case. How long before they figured out who was behind the identity theft? There was also an additional incentive attached to Marcus's death. He had a $200,000 insurance policy of which Lisa was the sole beneficiary. At the mention of the money, any scruples that Lallemand might have held, evaporated.

And so, Lallemand called up another of his associates, Jason Bucher, a young man who was both a talented counterfeiter and a skilled bomb maker. Bucher was the man who was tasked with constructing the bomb that ultimately took Marcus Toney's life. That bomb, as we now know, achieved its objective. But unfortunately for Lallemand, Bucher liked to boast of his achievements. Soon after the bombing, the Bureau of Alcohol, Tobacco, and Firearms (ATF) received a tip from one of its informants, naming Bucher as the bomb maker and Lallemand as his client. Bucher was immediately placed under surveillance but of Lallemand, there was no trace. He'd fled to Jamaica.

Given that Sienky Lallemand was now a fugitive from American justice, wanted for murder, and facing a possible death penalty if convicted, you might think that he would have kept a low profile in the Caribbean. But that would be to underestimate the audacity of a man like Lallemand. He was soon working the angles, posting a profile on a dating site and trawling for fresh blood. The woman he eventually snared was 54-year-old Sandra Lavel, an account executive with a Los Angeles movie studio.

Lavel accepted Lallemand's invitation to spend some time with him in Jamaica and flew out from L.A. The couple enjoyed four blissful days together at a Montego Bay resort, but those days passed all too quickly. Soon Lavel had to return to America. Already besotted with her young lover, she asked Lallemand to come and live with her in California. He said that he couldn't and told her why. He was a murder suspect. Most women would have run a mile on hearing this but not Sandra Lavel. She told him to come anyway, even promising to pay for plastic surgery, so that he could alter his appearance. Lallemand liked the idea. On March 22, he re-entered the United States, using a fake passport.

While all of this was going on, the ATF was continuing to keep Jason Bucher under surveillance. They knew that he was in e-mail contact with Lallemand but had thus far been unable to pin down Lallemand's location. Eventually, the agents decided to bring Bucher in and offer him a deal. He could hang tough and face a murder rap or he could cooperate with them and be allowed to plead to a lesser charge. Bucher took the deal. The response to his next e-mail was tracked to Sandra Laval's Los Angeles address. Within 24 hours, the fugitive was in custody. Lallemand was arrested while on his way to a plastic surgery appointment. One of his cheek implants had become infected.

The game was up for Sienky Lallemand and this time he was looking at a far harsher sentence than what he'd served before. The extenuating circumstances attached to the murder charge meant that he was eligible for the death penalty. The D.A. made it clear that he would be seeking that sanction unless Lallemand cooperated in the prosecution of Lisa Toney. Lisa had thus far denied involvement in her husband's murder, even though the evidence said otherwise. She had also taken a polygraph and failed. The investigators were sure that she had been the mastermind behind the bomb plot. Lallemand's statement indicated that they were right.

Of the accused, Sienky Lallemand, Jason Bucher, Sherri Payne, Sandra Laval, and another of Lallemand's accomplices, Jesse Jackson, all pleaded guilty and received varying sentences. Laval was also convicted of an unrelated crime. She had defrauded her employer of more than $1 million. The harshest sentence went to Lallemand, of course. He got life in prison. Bomb maker Jason Bucher was sentenced to fifteen years.

As for Lisa Toney, she continued to protest her innocence, right into the trial. She was convicted anyway and sentenced to life in prison. The sentence was later reduced on appeal to 25 years.

The Price

Carly and Leanne were sisters, two years between them, growing up in Brentwood, Essex during the 1990s. The girls were close, which made it doubly difficult when their parents split in 1994 and the sisters were separated. Carly, 8, went to live with her father; Leanne, two years younger, stayed with her mother. That would remain the status quo until three years later, when her mother met a man named Simon Meecham. Within just six weeks, she was walking down the aisle with him. Now Leanne had a stepfather. That was not, necessarily, a good thing.

Meecham was hardly a catch. He was tall and lanky with an unkempt appearance and a face that seemed perpetually drawn into a scowl. He was a heavy drinker and drug user, an auto mechanic by trade but usually unemployed. He was also a habitual criminal with a record that included over 100 arrests for charges relating to theft, to drugs, to public order offenses. Meecham fancied himself as a tough guy and was prone to using his fists on anyone who annoyed him. That included the women in his life. It wasn't long before his new wife was suffering the consequences.

Life inside the Meecham household was no picnic for Leanne and her mother. It was volatile, with frequent rows and numerous occasions when the police had to be called to restore order. And yet, Leanne appeared to be in awe of her stepfather. To friends, she boasted about how tough he was and how no one would mess with her for fear of him. She even insisted to her mother that she wanted to take her stepfather's surname. And that admiration appeared to be mutual. As Leanne grew into a pretty and vivacious teenager, her friends observed that the attention Meecham was paying her was not entirely paternal. They also noticed that he appeared jealous of any boy Leanne showed an interest in.

By March 2004, the situation on the home front had become so unstable that Leanne decided it was time to move out. She was 18 now and had a job and a steady boyfriend. And so, she moved into a small studio apartment and left the wars in the Meecham household behind her. A short while later, her mother and stepfather split up. That might have meant the end of Leanne's relationship with Simon, but he continued to call and visit. When she split with her boyfriend in 2007, he was there to catch her fall, a shoulder to cry on when she needed someone. It was then that he stated his true intention. He told her that he loved her and wanted to be with her.

One can only imagine how Leanne must have received this declaration of love. To her, Meecham was her father, the man who had raised her from the age of nine, the man who'd shared her mother's bed. But Leanne was also depressed and weak and vulnerable right now and Meecham took advantage of that.

Gradually, he won her over. In 2007, 20-year-old Leanne started a sexual relationship with her 36-year-old stepfather.

The affair, as you might imagine, was not well received by Leanne's family. But that played right into Meecham's hands. He soon persuaded Leanne to move with him to Southend-On-Sea, some twenty miles away. Then he convinced her to give up her job, saying that he had enough money to care for the both of them. In no time at all, he'd separated Leanne from her family and made her financially reliant on him. To a control freak like Meecham, this was as good as it got.

But still, it wasn't enough. Meecham also wanted Leanne to get drunk and high with him; he refused to let her study for the career in social work that she aspired to; he wanted to control who she connected with. On one occasion, he hacked her Facebook account and started unfriending people he didn't approve of. At other times, he exerted a more primitive form of control, using his fists on her. During 2010, the police were called to the couple's apartment on no fewer than six occasions. In the midst of this volatile situation, Leanne fell pregnant and delivered a baby, binding her even closer to her abusive lover.

The arrival of the child brought about a profound change in Leanne. It was time to grow up, time to give up the booze and the partying, time to revisit her dream of a career. She wanted to be a good mother. If (or more likely when) her relationship with Simon ended, she wanted to be able to provide for her child. Over the next couple of years, she would leave Meecham several times, although she always returned after he expressed repentance and promised to change. He never did, though, and it was only a matter of time before things reached breaking point.

That break came eventually on January 11, 2014, when Leanne called her sister Carly and asked if she and the baby could stay over for a few days. Meecham had beaten her up and had been arrested for assault. This time, Leanne, assured her sister, there was no way back.

Carly, of course, was happy to put her sister up. She was not quite so pleased when Leanne told her, just two days later, that she was returning to Southend. "I'm not going back to him," Leanne assured her. "But Southend is where I live now. I won't let him force me from my home."

And so, Leanne returned to her apartment, changing all the locks on the day that she arrived. That might have added to her sense of security, but she felt a lot less safe when Meecham was released on bail on January 29. Over the days that followed, Leanne would see him sitting in his car outside her apartment, watching her every move. Friends and family warned her to be careful, but Leanne was certain that he wouldn't harm her. Not with a court case pending for assault; not with a prison sentence hanging over his head. She was so certain that Meecham would keep his baser instincts at bay that she allowed him to visit, if only to see his child.

To Meecham, these visits were no more than a ruse. He had no interest in the baby. His real intention was to convince Leanne to take him back. Leanne, though, was adamant. It was over between them. She was moving on with her life. She was seeing someone else. You can only imagine how that news was received by Meecham. He started bombarding Leanne with texts and phone calls, begging her to come back to him. To a friend, he also made an ominous statement. If he couldn't have Leanne, then no one else would.

At around 9:30 a.m. on February 13, 2014, Leanne Meecham's neighbor saw Leanne's front door standing ajar and popped her head in to ensure that all was well. What she saw inside made her instantly recoil in horror. Then she was sprinting back to her apartment to call 999.

Police and emergency services were on the scene in mere minutes and arrived to a bloodbath. The walls of the hallway were splattered with blood and there were bloody handprints on the wall, apparently where Leanne had tried to hold herself upright. She'd not been able to do that, though. She'd collapsed to the floor and that was where the police found her, barely alive. She was transported to the nearest medical facility before being airlifted to the Royal London Hospital.

The prognosis was not good. Leanne had suffered two savage knife wounds, one to the neck, the other to the upper chest. Vital blood vessels had been severed and the resultant blood loss had triggered a cardiac arrest. She'd suffered brain damage due to a lack of oxygen. All that the doctors could do was to stabilize her condition and put her into a medically induced coma.

While all of this was playing out, police in Southend were hunting for Simon Meecham, believed to be responsible for the attack on Leanne. They found him in his Land Rover, parked at the seafront in Thorpe Bay. He too was injured, having suffered three stab wounds to the abdomen, one of which had perforated his liver. Police believed that these wounds were self-inflicted, although Meecham would tell a different story after he was treated for his injuries.

Meecham admitted that he had arrived at Leanne's apartment carrying a knife but insisted that he had brought it along because he wanted to kill himself in front of his former lover. However, Leanne had tried to prevent him from doing so and they'd tussled for control of the weapon. During that struggle, he'd been stabbed in the gut. Then he "swung his arm out to the side" and caught Leanne in the neck with the blade. "I did not even know that I was holding the knife," he claimed. "I only realized something was wrong when I saw the look of shock on her face."

This was a quite ludicrous story, and the police weren't buying it. Meecham was charged with attempted murder, a charge that was upgraded to murder when Leanne died a week later. Doctors had informed her family that there was no possibility that she would ever recover. They had then taken the heartbreaking decision to turn off life support.

Simon Meecham went on trial at Chelmsford Crown Court in August 2015. There, he entered a not guilty plea and spun the same ridiculous yarn about the murder being an accident. The jury was no more impressed by this story than the police had been. Meecham was found guilty and sentenced to life in prison. He must serve a minimum of 22 years before he is eligible for parole. His unseemly lust for his stepdaughter had come at a heavy cost. For her, the price was far, far greater.

Best Friends Forever

Doris Derryberry and Valerie Lane were best friends, inseparable, described by their families as "peas in a pod." Growing up in Marysville, California, during the early Seventies, the girls spent just about every waking moment in each other's company. They were doing just that on the morning of Sunday, November 11, 1973, visiting a local mall, buying some snacks at a donut shop, and then heading out to a roller rink. They were seen there, talking to another girl, in the parking lot at around 1 p.m. Then, mysteriously, they disappeared.

The girls' absence was not noticed until just after sunset. Thirteen-year-old Doris had a strict curfew in place. Her parents expected her home by the time the streetlights came on each evening. When she didn't appear, her slightly annoyed mom called Valerie's house. She was surprised to hear that Doris wasn't there, but it was the next piece of news that really set the alarm bells jangling. Valerie had told her mother that she would be having a sleepover at Doris's house.

Now followed a series of increasingly frantic phone calls, as both families worked the lines in an effort to track down the missing girls. Then, finally, some relief. One of the girls' friends said that she'd met them at the roller rink that afternoon and that they'd asked her to attend a party with them at Camp Far West Lake. So that was where they were, attending a teenage campout at the local beauty spot, some twenty miles out of town. Doris's sister immediately got into her car and drove there. Doris was going to be in some serious trouble when she got home.

Except that Doris and Valerie weren't at the lake. The party they'd wanted to attend was in full swing but there was no sign of either girl and none of the partygoers had seen them. It was time to call in the police. By daybreak, the Yuba County Sherriff's Office had launched a search for the teens. The first piece of intelligence they got was not promising. Someone had seen Doris and Valerie getting into a green pickup with two men.

And then, at around 1 p.m. on the afternoon of November 12, came the news everyone was dreading. Brothers Danny and Dwight Sullivan had been out hunting at Camp Far West when they'd come across the body of a young girl. Officers immediately raced to the scene and found the corpse as described, lying on her side next to a remote dirt road. It was evident that she'd been shot to death, most likely with a shotgun. However, she had not died instantly. A clump of grass clutched in her hand suggested that she had tried to crawl away before succumbing to her injuries. An officer searched her pockets and found a school paper with her name on it. It was Valerie Lane.

Valerie Lane's life clock had been stopped at just twelve years and the police did not hold out much hope of finding her friend Doris alive. Sadly, that would prove to be the case. Doris was found just 35 feet away, on the other side of a small incline. She was lying on her back, her abdomen ripped apart by what appeared to be a shotgun blast. From the extent of the injuries, officers surmised that her killer had stood over the girl and cold-bloodedly executed her as she cowered in the dirt. An autopsy would later reveal that Doris's shoulder had also been dislocated and that she had been raped.

So who might have committed such a heinous crime against two little girls? The first clue was a name, scrawled in pen on Doris's stomach, "Robert C." Asked about this, the dead girl's sister said that she thought it might refer to Robert Clark, a boy in Doris's class who she'd had a crush on. Clark was brought in for questioning but was ultimately cleared. He did own a shotgun, but the ballistics didn't match the shell casings found at the scene.

While Robert Clark was being investigated and dismissed as a suspect, another team of investigators was trying to track down the green pickup that the girls were seen getting into. This was an important lead because Doris's family was adamant that she would not have accepted a ride from a stranger. That narrowed the field somewhat. Everyone with even a tenuous connection to the family was investigated but, in the end, the search for the truck came up empty.

The next move by investigators was to re-interview the brothers who'd found the body. There are numerous cases on record where the killer turns out to be the person who reported the crime. Not in this case, however. The brothers were adamant that they'd done nothing but their civic duty. Ballistics would prove that they were telling the truth. The same technology would also clear over 200 gun owners whose weapons were tested.

Ask any homicide detective about a case that he or she could not let go and invariably you will find a child murder at the top of the list. Yet, despite the determination of Yuma County law officers to bring the perpetrator to justice, this case seemed to be slipping away. Desperate, investigators began looking into the possibility that the Zodiac, one of California's most infamous serial killers, might be responsible. This connection was based on a rather tenuous link. In a letter written to the San Francisco Chronicle years earlier, the notorious killer had written, "I love killing people because it's more fun than killing animals in the forest." This long-shot idea would end up going nowhere. Inevitably, the case went cold. It would remain so for over four decades.

More than forty years later, in March 2014, the Derryberry/Lane case file landed on the desk of Yuba County cold case investigator Karen Howard. Det. Howard had grown up in the Marysville area and had been roughly the same age as Doris and Valerie back when the case was in the headlines. She could still remember the pall of fear that had hung over the town for years after. That gave the case a special significance to her. Yet, despite the near-mythical status afforded to cold case detectives on TV, Howard was acutely aware that closing such a case is very much a hit-or-miss affair. It all comes down to the work done by the original investigators. How methodical were they in gathering and labeling evidence? What steps did they take to preserve biological samples? How much evidence had there been to gather, in the first place?

In this case, there was plenty, and the investigative team had been thorough indeed. Howard submitted sperm samples as well as the clothing that the victims had been wearing on the day that they were killed. Then she waited. Finally, in December 2015, she had a reply, not one but two DNA profiles had been extracted. Even better news was to come from CODIS, the FBI's national DNA database. There was a match on both samples. The men that Detective Howard was looking for were named William Lloyd Harbour and Larry Don Patterson.

Delving deeper into the background of these men, Howard learned that they were cousins and that they had both lived within a few hundred yards of the Derryberry family at the time of the murders. Harbour was well-known to local law enforcement as a methamphetamine dealer; Patterson had a record for sexual assault. Both men had been 22 years old at the time of the murders and would be in their mid-sixties now. Harbour still lived in the area, while Patterson's current whereabouts were unknown. He would be traced, eventually, to Oklahoma. In the meantime, the police held off on arresting Harbour but kept him under surveillance.

The reason for this was obvious. Had they moved in and arrested Harbour, he might have gotten word to Patterson, allowing him to go on the run. The only way to avoid that happening was to take both men into custody at the same time. Finally, in September 2016, the police were in a position to do so. Harbour and Patterson were taken down in coordinated raids, four states apart. After 43 years, justice had caught up with them.

Once in custody, the men employed very different strategies. Harbour flat out denied that he'd had anything to do with the murders while Patterson clammed up and refused to say a word. But Patterson's tongue loosened considerably on the long drive from Oklahoma to California. By the time he arrived back in Yuba County, he was singing like a bird.

That is not to say that he was telling the truth, though. According to Patterson, he and Harbour had picked up the girls hitchhiking and had promised them a ride to Camp Far West. However, they'd just entered the park when Harbour pulled over to the side of the road and suggested that they "get the party started." Patterson had then taken Doris into the bushes where, he claimed, they had consensual sex. When they returned to the truck, he saw Harbour struggling in the cab with Valerie. Doris then agreed to have sex with Harbor, to spare her friend.

Patterson went on to say that it had never been their intention to kill the girls. However, Doris had made a run for it and Harbour had then told him to shoot her. He said that he'd fired but missed and Harbour had then killed both of the girls. He, in other words, was completely blameless, other than for the statutory rape of a 13-year-old.

But Patterson's story did not hold up to the evidence. Firstly, his story that Doris had consented to sex was ludicrous. The girl had quite obviously put up a fight. Her shoulder had even been dislocated in the process. Additionally, her clothes had been ripped. This was not indicative of someone who had given her permission. It would also have been impossible for Harbour to have shot both victims. The girls had run in opposite directions and were found 35 feet apart. That suggested that each of the men must have shot one of the girls. The police believed that it was Harbour who shot Valerie while Patterson was the one who'd stood over Doris and cold-bloodedly executed her.

The Derryberry and Lane families had spent over four decades mourning their lost children, praying for the day that they would see justice done. When that day arrived, it would be a bitter disappointment. The case against the killers was strong forensically but weak in other respects. Many witnesses, including some of the original investigators, had died in the intervening years. Under these circumstances, putting the case before a jury was considered a risk by prosecutors. It was therefore decided to offer a deal to the defendants, allowing them to plead to second-degree murder. Harbour and Patterson, of course, jumped at the chance.

But that wasn't even the worst of it. Prosecutors had to abide by the sentencing guidelines that were in place at the time of the murders. These stipulated a term of five years to life. William Harbour and Larry Patterson will be eligible for parole after serving a paltry 60 months behind bars. Given that they will both be in their seventies by then, there is every chance that they will walk free at the first time of asking. That hardly feels like justice at all.

A Woman Scorned

Dr. Herman Tarnower wasn't much to look at. In his late sixties and with a balding head, beak nose, and a somewhat gaunt appearance, he was hardly the kind of man to set a lady's heart aflutter. Still, the doctor was rich, and he was a minor celebrity, the author of a New York Times bestseller, *The Scarsdale Diet*. Perhaps that is what attracted women to him because, despite his looks, Dr. Tarnower had a reputation as a ladies' man. By the time that our story takes place, in March 1980, the good doctor had left a string of lovers in his wake. One of those was the principal of a prestigious school for girls in Washington D.C. Her name was Jean Harris.

Jean Harris was born Jean Struven in Cleveland, Ohio in 1923. Her mother was a religious fanatic who followed the fringe Christian Scientist movement. Her father, Albert, was a talented engineer who was plagued by bipolar disorder and anger management issues. This, as you might imagine, did not make for a very nurturing home environment. Jean, nonetheless, was an outstanding student who went on to attend Smith College, a private liberal arts school for women in Northampton, Massachusetts. She emerged from her time there with a degree in economics. Shortly after graduation, she walked down the aisle with a handsome Navy veteran named Jim Harris. The couple settled into a comfortable home in Grosse Pointe, Michigan, and were blessed with two sons over the next two years. However, the marriage would eventually fail and by 1965, Jean was back on the market. Now in her early forties, she was still a very attractive woman. It was hardly a surprise that she caught the eye of Dr. Herman Tarnower.

Herman Tarnower was Brooklyn-born and bred. An intelligent child, he graduated at the top of his class and went on to study medicine, eventually setting himself up as a cardiologist in the Scarsdale and White Plains areas of New York. Then World War II intervened and Dr. Tarnower was co-opted into the US Army Medical Corps where he would rise to the rank of major. After the conclusion of hostilities, he established the Scarsdale Medical Center and soon became well-known for his unique approach to treating coronary disease. Dr. Tarnower was a strong proponent of the 'food as medicine' philosophy, an idea that is commonplace nowadays but was quite groundbreaking at the time. Away from his surgery, the good doctor was quite the socialite, hosting elaborate dinner parties that were a much-coveted invitation among New York's upper echelons.

Tarnower was also the quintessential bachelor, a predatory womanizer with a love-em-and-leave-em attitude. It was therefore a surprise to everyone when, shortly after meeting Jean Harris, he asked her to marry him. Jean said no, citing the fact that it would mean uprooting her sons from school. She did hint, however, that she might be more amenable if he popped the question again at the end of the academic year, when a move would be less disruptive for the boys. Unfortunately for Jean, Tarnower had moved on by then. He no longer wanted to commit to her. In fact, he now suggested that they maintain an open relationship and see other people.

Jean Harris never did take her lover's advice. She remained devoted to him over the next 14 years, while he continued to tomcat around, playing with her affections. Jean didn't like it, but she stayed because she believed that any affair he embarked on was short-term and that he'd always return to her. And that was generally true during the first decade-and-a-half that they were together. But then there was Lynne Tryforos, an attractive medical assistant at the Scarsdale Clinic. Tarnower immediately set about seducing the young woman and soon bedded her. But this was no two-week fling. He seemed genuinely smitten with Lynne. Even more galling for Jean was the fact that Lynne was 20 years younger than her and that all of Dr. Tarnower's friends seemed to like her.

And her failing love affair wasn't the only thing playing on Jean Harris's mind at that time. In the mid-seventies, she'd embarked on a new career path, entering the realm of academia as the Director of Springside Middle School, an exclusive girls' only college in Philadelphia. She'd done spectacularly well in that role, so much so that she attracted the attention of an even more prestigious institution, the Madeira School for Girls in Washington D.C. Despite its stellar reputation, though, the Madeira School was in decline when Harris took over in 1977. Her remit was to bring it back to its former glory. That, however, would prove a bridge too

far for Principal Harris. After failing to make any headway during
her first two years on the job, her position was in serious jeopardy.
By May 1979, the board of trustees was discussing the termination
of her contract.

In the midst of all this, Harris' personal life was in turmoil. A war
had broken out between her and Lynne Tryforos, over the
affections of Dr. Tarnower. The two women frequently exchanged
insults and harassing phone calls. They also destroyed or damaged
any property belonging to the other that was left behind at
Tarnower's house. On one occasion, Jean arrived for a weekend
visit and found her favorite dress smeared with excrement. Her
response was to make a series of late-night calls to her rival,
keeping them up for over a month. Such behavior takes a toll,
though. Jean was struggling to cope, sinking deeper and deeper
into depression, relying heavily on the methamphetamines that Dr.
Tarnower prescribed for her. She was also thinking seriously
about suicide.

And then came the incident that would finally push Jean Harris
over the edge. It happened on March 7, 1980, when the Dean of the
Madeira School carried out a dormitory inspection and found
marijuana paraphernalia in the rooms of four students. Harris was
informed and acted decisively by expelling the girls. This was
totally in line with her remit to restore the school's reputation. She
could not have imagined the backlash that it would elicit. First, she
found herself confronted by angry parents. Then she was called in
by the board and raked over the coals for 'overreacting'. Finally,
the entire student body came out in protest against the treatment
of the 'Madeira Four.' Even one of Harris' favorite students
condemned her for the expulsions, writing a letter of complaint. In

Jean Harris's fragile emotional state this was the last straw. The following day, she purchased a .32 revolver. Her intention was to kill herself.

On Saturday, March 8, Harris sat down and wrote a long rambling letter to Dr. Tarnower chronicling the many wrongs she felt had been inflicted on her. She also criticized Lynne Tryforos, describing her rival in unflattering terms and accusing her of ruining her clothes and stealing items of her jewelry. In the same letter, she admitted that she was not without blame and that she'd also destroyed items of Tryforos's property. The letter ended with a plea for Tarnower to "treat her better." It was posted the same day.

But as soon as the envelope dropped through the slot, Harris regretted sending it. After fretting over it for the rest of the weekend, she phoned Tarnower on Monday, May 10, asking him not to read the letter and to destroy it unopened. Tarnower agreed to do so and then acceded to another request. He agreed to meet with her later that day. That meeting would require Harris to make a 5-hour drive. She left right away, bringing her newly acquired .32 with her.

According to Harris's later testimony, she made the trip that day with only one purpose in mind. She wanted to see Dr. Tarnower one last time before killing herself. She planned to say her farewells to her lover and then to row out to a small island on a pond on Tarnower's property, a location she described as her favorite place. There she would end her life.

But things didn't turn out that way. On arriving at the estate, Harris found Tarnower in a particularly uncaring mood. He didn't want to talk to her and ignored her pleas to sit down and discuss their relationship. Then Harris came across some of her rival's things, including a negligee, and that sent her into a rage. She started throwing the objects around the room and now, at last, she got a response from Tarnower. "Jesus, Jean, you're crazy! Get out of here!" he shouted. He then walked across and tried to force her from the room. During the altercation that followed, he slapped her face. That was when she pulled the gun.

According to Harris, she'd only drawn the weapon to fulfill her intention of killing herself. But Tarnower tried the wrestle the gun from her, and it accidentally discharged – five times! Tarnower was hit and slumped to the floor, bleeding from several wounds. Then Jean turned the gun on herself, but the hammer clicked on an empty chamber. She'd used up all her bullets shooting her lover. By the time police and paramedics arrived on the scene, Dr. Herman Tarnower was already dead.

The trial of Jean Harris began at the Westchester County Court in December 1980. It would last for three months and become a national obsession, covered by media outlets from coast to coast. Harris entered a not guilty plea and cited temporary insanity. She continued to insist that the shooting had been accidental.

But the evidence was strongly against her. Forensics experts argued that Dr. Tarnower had been asleep when the first shot was fired. He'd then put up his hand in a futile attempt to protect himself and had suffered a defensive wound before Harris pumped three more bullets into his prone body. This was not an accidental shooting. It was an assassination.

Also entered into evidence was the 10-page letter that Harris had written to her victim, the one she'd asked him to destroy. This was read out in court, and it was shocking, showing an unexpected side to Harris's character. In it, she described her rival, Lynne Tryforos, in terms that would have made a sailor blush. The media lapped it up, of course. The idea that a prim and proper school principal was capable of such vulgarity is the stuff that sensational news stories are made of. It also did Harris's cause no good. After deliberating for eight days, the jury returned a guilty verdict to second-degree murder. Harris was subsequently sentenced to 15 years to life and confined at the Bedford Hills Correctional Facility in Westchester County, New York.

Harris would prove to be a model prisoner, setting up a program to help inmates further their education and also starting a nursery for babies born to convict moms. In the meantime, she lodged several appeals, but all of these were rejected. She was eventually released in 1992, on grounds of ill-health, after she suffered two heart attacks. One of the first things she did after gaining her freedom was to visit Herman Tarnower's grave at Mount Hope Cemetery in Hastings-on-Hudson. She would visit several more times over the coming years.

Jean Harris died of natural causes on December 23, 2012. She was 89 years old. Her case has inspired several books and two movies, one of which starred Annette Benning as Harris and Ben Kingsley as Dr. Tarnower.

Who Killed Jill Dando?

At around 11:30 on the morning of April 26, 1999, British TV personality Jill Dando arrived at her home in Fulham, London. Pulling her BMW convertible to the curb, the 37-year-old got out, rummaging through her bag for her house keys as she walked the short distance to her front gate. Ms. Dando had recently moved from the address, taking up residence with her fiancée, Dr. Alan Farthing, in nearby Chiswick. She'd only come to the Fulham terrace to pick up some things. She had no idea that someone was tracking her as she approached the front door.

The man acted quickly and decisively, walking up behind Dando on cushioned feet. He grabbed her by the scruff of the neck just as she slotted her key into the lock and forced her to her knees on her own doorstep, pushing her head down until her nose was almost touching the ground. Then he had a 9mm pistol in his hand, pointed at her left temple, held so close that the muzzle made contact with her skin. Without uttering a word, he pulled the trigger, discharging a single bullet into her skull just above the left ear. A projectile fired at this range causes terrible damage to the human body. The bullet chewed through bone and brain matter, wreaking havoc before it exited on the other side. The thud of the pistol was muted, lost in the normal morning din of suburbia. It went wholly unnoticed as the shooter allowed his victim to collapse to the ground, dark blood already welling up into her short-cut blonde hair. Then he walked away, disappearing into the anonymity of the big city.

Jill Dando's body was found a short while later, when a near neighbor walked past her house and spotted her lying on the ground. A 999 call brought police and paramedics racing to the scene, but it was already too late for the latter to be of any use. The much-loved TV presenter of Holiday, Crimewatch, Breakfast Time, and BBC News was dead, assassinated on a London street. Now it was up to the police to find her killer.

And the Metropolitan Police left no stone unturned in their quest to do that, launching the largest criminal investigation in the UK since the hunt for the Yorkshire Ripper. Over the months that followed, they would record thousands of statements, trace 1,200 cars and investigate nearly 2,000 potential suspects. The initial theory was that Dando had been killed over some romantic entanglement. She'd certainly had an interesting love life, including relationships with a BBC producer and with a South African game ranger several years her junior. There'd also been several short-term flings. Perhaps TV's golden girl had trampled on someone's feelings, someone like the Russian crime boss who had tried, and failed, to lure her to his bed.

Dando had met the man while she was in Cyprus filming an episode of the travel program, Holiday. Apparently, he'd been besotted with her and keen on pursuing a relationship. But Jill had rejected his advances, leaving him disappointed and angry. Angry enough to order a hit on her? That seemed like a stretch and the police also came to disregard the idea that a spurned lover or romantic rival could have done this. A new theory had emerged, one that stemmed from Ms. Dando's work on another BBC program.

On April 6, 1999, just twenty days before her death, Jill Dando had fronted a BBC fundraiser for victims of ethnic cleansing in the Balkans. The Kosovo Crisis Appeal had raised over £1 million in 24 hours. Two weeks later, on the night of 23-24 April 1999, British and US warplanes had bombed the Radio Television Serbia building in Belgrade, killing sixteen of the news organization's employees. The following day, BBC news head Tony Hall received an odd phone call. Speaking in a heavy East European accent, the caller had informed him, "Your prime minister Blair butchered innocent young people, we butcher back." Two days later, Jill Dando would be dead.

So did some Serbian warlord – generally touted to be the notorious militia leader Arkan – dispatch a hitman on a revenge mission? Did he decide to strike back at the woman who just weeks earlier had been the face of "western propaganda" against his country? As far-fetched as it seems, this theory had plenty of traction. The efficiency of the killing suggested a professional hit and the call to the BBC seems ominous. But that call was later decried as a hoax and there are elements of the killing that suggest that the shooter might not have been a pro after all. Trained assassins prefer small caliber weapons that make less noise and are easier to conceal. They usually "double-tap" their victims – two shots to the head rather than one. They also do not leave shell casings at the scene, as this killer had done. These things tended to mitigate against a professional shooter.

And yet the notion of a hired gun refused to go away. A new tweak on the theory suggested that the hitman might have been acting on behalf of a shadowy figure in the London underworld. According to this hypothesis, Jill Dando had been killed because of her work as the presenter of Crimewatch. On the face of it, this seems like an even weaker proposal than the earlier one. Jill Dando's TV work was hardly going to make her a target. She was disseminating information, not acting as some crusading crime fighter. If there was some criminal mastermind out for revenge, he'd be far more likely to seek out police informants. He might even target senior police officers or bothersome detectives. The death of a TV personality, even the presenter of Britain's foremost crime program, hardly seems worth the risk.

Still, investigators took the idea seriously enough to interview around thirty criminals who had been run to ground as a result of tip-offs generated by Crimewatch. They also interviewed a number of convicted hitmen in prison, hoping to generate some leads in the case. In the end, they came up empty and the hitman theory was laid to rest. The focus had now shifted to a lone random gunman, a stalker, a stranger on the street. This idea was first proffered by forensic criminal psychologist Dr. Adrian West, who urged police to look for an "obsessive loner." They found him in the form of 58-year-old Barry George.

George had, in fact, been mentioned to investigators in the very first days of the murder inquiry. He was said to be "mentally unstable," a fantasist who sometimes told people that his name was Paul Gadd (the real name of disgraced pop star Gary Glitter). At other times, George claimed that he was Barry Bulsara, the cousin of the late Queen singer, Freddie Mercury. While these might seem like harmless flights of fantasy, there was a dark side to Barry George, too.

Several women had lodged stalking complaints against him, and he also had a criminal record for attempted rape, for indecent assault, and for trespass. That latter charge related to an incident in the early 1980s when George was discovered hiding on the grounds of Kensington Palace, the London residence of Princess Eugenie. George was dressed in camouflage gear and was found to be carrying a knife and a length of rope, at that time. He also had experience with firearms, having spent a year in the Territorial Army. And he lived just 500 yards from Jill Dando's Fulham residence.

And yet, despite all of this, it took the police ten months before they eventually got around to taking Barry George seriously as a suspect. When they did, they searched his apartment and found dozens of photographs he'd taken of local women. They also found no fewer than four copies of Ariel magazine's Jill Dando memorial issue. An even more damning piece of evidence was a tiny trace of gunshot residue, found in George's overcoat pocket. The suspect offered several versions of how the residue might have gotten there, none of them verified by the facts. Finally, there was eyewitness testimony that placed George in the vicinity of Jill Dando's house on the day she was shot.

Barry George was arrested and charged with murder. He was put on trial at the Old Bailey in June 2001 and convicted by a majority 10-1 verdict on July 2. The sentence of the court was life in prison, but George appealed and in 2007 had his conviction overturned. In truth, he probably should not have been convicted in the first place.

At George's second trial, in 2008, his defense homed in on one thing. The killer of Jill Dando had acted with cold, calculated efficiency. This was not a random shooting; this was a professionally planned and expertly executed assassination. With an IQ of 75, putting him in the lowest five percent of the population, George simply lacked the mental capacity to have done what he was accused of. As for the forensic evidence produced at the first trial, the defense put a firearms expert on the stand who testified that the source of the residue found in George's pocket was impossible to determine. There was no science in existence that could say, without reasonable doubt, that it was from the gun that had killed Jill Dando.

It was no surprise to anyone that Barry George was acquitted the second time around. But mere acquittal wasn't enough for George. He rightly wanted reparation for false arrest, for false imprisonment, for seven wasted years spent behind bars. He would take his complaint all the way to the High Court where his case was inexplicably rejected in 2013. George may have been acquitted of murder but, in the opinion of the court, he would only qualify for compensation if new evidence emerged that proved beyond reasonable doubt that he had not committed the offense. It seems a strange reversal of the 'innocent until proven guilty' standard. Or, as George himself put it, "It seems that I am innocent but not innocent enough."

Two decades on from the murder of Jill Dando, the case remains unsolved. It seems we may never know who gunned down the BBC's golden girl, or why.

Prodigal Son

To those who knew Harry Kendall Thaw, even those who held him near and dear, there was never any doubt that he'd come to a bad end. Born in Pittsburgh, Pennsylvania, on February 12, 1871, Harry was the son of coal and railroad baron William Thaw. He was raised with every advantage in life. And yet, Harry was trouble almost from the time he could walk. He grew to be a disruptive and callous youth, one who bounced from one fancy private school to another. But for his father's wealth and influence, he would probably have ended up in a reformatory.

That was never going to happen, of course. Not when William Thaw had connections stretching all the way to the White House. Despite a less than stellar academic record, Harry was granted admission to the University of Pittsburgh. There he studied law, although "studied" is a bit of a stretch. Most of his time was spent gambling and drinking, attending cockfights, and chasing women. He then decided that UPJ was below his social standard and demanded that his father pull some strings to get him into Harvard. Thaw the elder obliged, of course. He'd do anything for his son. But Harry's tenure in Cambridge would be a brief one. He was expelled from the school after being arrested for threatening a cab driver with a shotgun. His argument that the weapon had not been loaded carried little weight with the disciplinary board.

After his expulsion from Harvard, Harry Thaw drifted to New York, where he developed an addiction to cocaine and a liking for chorus line girls. It was also during this time that Thaw met the man who would become his nemesis, famed architect Stanford White, the designer of several New York landmarks, including Madison Square Garden. White had similar proclivities to Thaw, and an undeclared war flared up between the two. At stake were the tenuous affections of various young dancers and it was a war that White was winning. When most of the young women started giving Thaw the cold shoulder, he blamed it on his rival, saying that White was spreading ugly rumors about him. He then swore revenge and saw his opportunity when White fell for Evelyn Nesbit, a chorus line girl on the Broadway show Florodora. If he could steal her away, he reasoned, he would have inflicted a hurtful blow on his rival.

Unfortunately for Thaw, White got wind of his plans and warned Evelyn to stay away from him. For weeks, Thaw tried to pin her down to a dinner date, only to be snubbed at every turn. Then fate took a turn in his favor. Evelyn was struck down by appendicitis and admitted to hospital. Learning of this, Thaw paid her a visit, bearing flowers and other gifts. Over the days that followed, he became a regular visitor and was so attentive that he even won over Evelyn's mother. Later, when the young woman was moved to a sanatorium in upstate New York, he continued to call on her. White also kept up his visits and a farcical situation developed in which the two men tried to outdo one another in their devotion to Evelyn. But while White eventually lost interest, Thaw did not. The truth of the matter was that he'd fallen for Evelyn Nesbit.

With Stanford White out of the picture, Thaw had a clear run at Evelyn. Shortly after her release from the hospital, he invited her and her mother to accompany him on a trip to Paris. During that excursion, he asked Evelyn to marry him and was surprised when she turned him down. However, Thaw was used to getting his way in life and would not be easily denied. For several weeks, he continued to press until one night Evelyn broke down and explained the reason for her refusal. She had surrendered her virginity to Stanford White, she said, and was therefore unworthy of being his wife.

Thaw was apoplectic at this revelation. He raged over it for several days before eventually regaining his composure. Then he sat Evelyn down and told her that his feelings for her were undiminished. Despite her liaison with his rival, he still wanted to marry her. Evelyn again refused him, but she did agree to travel with him to Germany, while her mother returned to New York. It was in a Bavarian castle that Thaw and Evelyn were first intimate, although this was no romantic encounter. After beating her with a dog whip, Thaw insisted that she recount the intimate details of her relationship with Stanford White. He then forced himself on her and took what had thus far been denied to him.

Given her treatment at the hands of Harry Thaw, you might have expected Evelyn Nesbit to flee from him the minute they were back on American soil. But Evelyn did no such thing. Perhaps she was afraid of Thaw, aware that he had the resources to track her down, wherever she might run. Or perhaps the idea of being courted by one of New York's wealthiest, most eligible bachelors held some appeal. In any case, she stayed, endured the beatings, and recounted on demand the stories of her sexual encounters with Stanford White. She also continued to turn down Thaw's marriage proposals until Thaw, in desperation, sent his mother to talk to her. Mrs. Thaw begged her to accept, saying that marriage would be good for Harry and might help to curb his eccentricities. Eventually, Evelyn was persuaded. The couple married on April 4, 1905.

This, however, would be no happily ever after. With Evelyn now secured as another of his "possessions," Harry lost interest in her. Often, he'd disappear for weeks on end, offering no explanation when he eventually returned. When he was around, Evelyn would have to endure the worst of his sadomasochistic inclinations. She would also have to recount endless retellings of her first night with Stanford White. This oft-repeated tale never failed to send Thaw into a rage. Nonetheless, it seemed almost as though he enjoyed being hurt by his wife's words. The woman he loved had been deflowered by the man he hated. Even after all this time, his loathing for Stanford White was undiminished.

In the spring of 1906, the Thaws traveled to New York, where they were to board a luxury liner bound for Europe. On the evening of June 25, they were dining at Cafe Martin when they spotted Stanford White at a nearby table. White was regaling his guests with a story about Mam'zelle Champagne, a show that they were to attend that evening. As it turned out, the Thaws had tickets for the same show. They left without finishing their meals, returning to their hotel. There, Thaw told Evelyn to wait until he came back for her. He was gone for over an hour, returning with just enough time for them to make the curtain. To Evelyn's surprise, her husband was wearing a long, black overcoat, despite the humidity of the evening. She knew better than to ask.

Mam'zelle Champagne was showing at the rooftop theatre of Madison Square Garden. This was a dinner theater, with guests seated at round, restaurant-style tables. There was a full house that night, with both the Thaws and Stanford White seated near the stage. Thaw was still wearing his long coat, which he'd refused to hand over at the hat check. Sweat had formed on his brow and he seemed distracted, fidgety. Several times during the performance, he got out of his seat and took a few steps towards Stanford White before returning to his seat. Now, with the cast performing the finale, "I Could Love a Million Girls," he got up again and strode towards White's table. His hand went into his coat and came out holding a revolver. As White looked up in surprise, Thaw pulled the trigger.

Three shots rang out in the crowded theater. At first, there was a smattering of laughter from the audience, who no doubt thought that this was part of the show. But then a woman let out a shrill scream, sparking a stampede towards the exits. In the midst of this melee stood Harry Thaw, looking impassively at his rival who was face down on the table, his blood spreading out across the pristine, white linen. Shot three times in the face at point-blank range, White never stood a chance.

Harry Thaw was waiting calmly at the theater when the police arrived. Arrested and charged with murder, he would face two trials. The first of these ended in a hung jury. At the second, Harry entered an insanity plea, and the Thaw family made an offer to Evelyn. If she would testify that Stanford White had abused her and that Harry had acted in her interests, she could divorce Harry and walk away with $1 million in compensation. Evelyn agreed and performed admirably on the stand. Her testimony played a significant part in the verdict – not guilty by reason of insanity. Harry was sent to the Matteawan State Hospital for the Criminally Insane in Fishkill, New York, and Evelyn got her divorce. However, the Thaw family reneged on the financial compensation that had been offered. Evelyn did not see a cent.

The unconventional life of Harry K. Thaw did not end with his incarceration. In 1913, he escaped the hospital and fled to Canada, although he was later arrested there and extradited to the United States. In 1916, shortly after his release, he was accused of kidnapping, sexually assaulting, and horsewhipping a teenaged boy to within an inch of his life. That saw him returned to confinement. After his release, in 1924, he became a movie producer, although his short career would be beset by conflict and litigation. In 1944, he retired to Miami, Florida. He died there three years later, at the age of 76.

Evelyn Nesbit's life after her divorce from Harry Thaw would also be eventful. In 1910, Evelyn had given birth to a son, who she named Russell William Thaw. She claimed that the boy had been conceived during a conjugal visit, but Harry Thaw denied paternity and the Thaw family never acknowledged the child as one of their own. Russell Thaw would go on to become a skilled aviator and a WWII flying ace.

Over the years that followed, Evelyn worked at various jobs. She was, variously, the proprietor of a tearoom, a dancer in a burlesque review, a silent movie actress, and a ceramics instructor. She served as a consultant on the Hollywood movie, "The Girl on the Red Velvet Swing," a sensationalized version of her life story. She remarried and divorced. In 1926, while recovering from a suicide attempt in a Chicago Hospital, she was visited by Harry Thaw. There was media talk of a reunion, but it never happened. Evelyn Nesbit died in Santa Monica, California, on January 17, 1967, at the age of 82.

Along Came Joe

Tania Herman

On the evening of Friday, August 12, 2005, police in Melbourne, Australia fielded a couple of 000 calls in quick succession. The first was from a newspaper journalist, the second from a rather distraught woman. Both reported the same thing. They'd just been called by a man named Joe Korp who had told them that he was about to hang himself in the garage at his home. The female caller was Korp's ex-wife, and she was able to give the dispatcher his address, in the Melbourne suburb of Mickleham.

Units rushed to the scene. They arrived to find the residence securely locked. Peering through a slot in the garage door, they could see a man standing on a ladder, a noose around his neck, the other end tied to a ceiling beam. Then the man appeared to lose his balance. He tried to regain it, but failed, slipping from his perch. As the officers watched helplessly, the man throttled to death at the end of the rope.

Joe Korp was well-known to the police. He was currently embroiled in a highly publicized case, involving the death of his wife. Maria Korp had been buried that very day, after lingering for five months in a coma. Her condition was the result of an attempt on her life by her husband's lover, a woman named Tania Herman. Herman was now serving a 12-year term and the word was that Korp was about to be charged with murder. Now he'd circumvented the process by hanging himself. He'd died surrounded by photographs of his dead wife. He'd also left behind a note declaring his love for Maria and swearing that he was innocent of her murder.

So how had it come to this, with a wife murdered and her husband hanging himself in the garage? To answer that question, we must first peek into the life of the other key player in this melodrama, the lover, Tania Herman.

Tania Herman was born in Rochester, Victoria in 1966. She was the youngest of four children and appears to have had a happy, stable early childhood. But then, when she was just six years old, she was sexually assaulted by an adult man. This abuse would continue until she was twelve and would set off a pattern in Tania's life, exposing her to a succession of manipulative, abusive men. The first of those was John Linton, who she married at 17 and divorced within five months. Then there was a two-year romance with a Columbian student which produced a daughter but ended after she caught him in bed with another woman. Then there was Paul Herman, a charter boat operator from Queensland. They married in 1996 and had a daughter together. But by 2002, the marriage was over. Paul was drinking heavily and had become physically abusive. He eventually died of a heart attack, brought on by his alcoholism.

At around this time, Tania was dealing with her own health issues. She'd been diagnosed with cervical cancer and was receiving chemotherapy and radiation treatment. This caused her to lose her hair, but Tania was not ready to share the details of her condition with anyone. When her family asked, she said that she had shaved her head voluntarily, to raise money for a cancer charity.

By October 2003, Tania's cancer was in remission and her blond locks had grown back. But there was still a hole in her life that she was desperate to fill. She wanted a new relationship, one with a man who wouldn't cheat on her, beat her, or lose himself in the bottle. Since all of her previous attempts at finding Mr. Right had failed, she decided on a new strategy. She would conduct her search for love on the web. That was how she met Joe Korp. Joe was shopping his affections online under the handle JoeK40. His profile stated that he was a self-employed building contractor, aged 40, and currently single. The truth was that he was 45, worked in a factory, and was very much married, to his second wife, Maria.

Tania, of course, knew none of this. All she knew was that JoeK40 was attractive, that he was financially independent, and that he seemed like a good prospect. After trading messages online, they spoke on the phone a few times before agreeing to meet in person. That meeting took place on February 11, 2004. It started with lunch in the city center and ended with sex in the back of Joe's car, down by the Murray River. After that first encounter, Tania was smitten. So too, apparently, was Joe.

Over the next few months, the couple would often spend weekends together. Joe would tell Maria that he had to travel to Sydney for business and would then drive to Tania's house in nearby Echuca. It is uncertain when she found out that he had been lying about his marital status but by then it was too late. Tania was deeply in love. Besides, the way that Joe spun it, his home life was a living hell. He told her that his marriage was loveless and sexless and described his wife as neurotic and possessive. According to him, she'd threatened frequently to stab him while he slept. He'd leave her, he said, but she had some information on him, information that would land him in prison should it ever get out.

Tania was desperate to believe, so desperate that she bought every lie that Joe Korp told her. What she didn't know was that he was still playing the internet dating game, spinning one lie after another as he hooked up with other women for sex. One particularly callous falsehood had Tania believing that her lover had been killed in a car wreck in Barcelona. Then, as she grieved, he reappeared, telling her that the details had been misreported, that he'd only been injured. That episode left her more devoted to him than ever. When he started hinting that the only way for them to be together was to murder his wife, she barely blinked.

And so, a plot was hatched. In typical Joe Korp fashion, it involved no risk on his part. Various methods were discussed, including killing Maria in a hit-and-run and in a faked burglary. The plan they eventually settled on was far less convoluted. Tania would enter the house and strangle Maria. It was the only way, Joe told her. He could not be directly involved since he'd be the first person the police would suspect. He needed to be elsewhere to establish an alibi.

On the morning of February 9, 2005, Joe Korp went down to his garage and opened the door allowing Tania to sneak in. He then went back inside and had breakfast with his wife. In the meantime, Tania donned a ski mask and cotton gloves and readied herself for what was to come. Finally, at around 6:20, Korp left for work. On his way out, he hugged Tania and told her that he loved her. "You're doing this for us," he assured her. "Don't let the bitch get out of here alive." Then he drove away, leaving his wife to her fate.

But Tania did not follow through immediately with the plan. For about ten minutes, she crouched in the dark, uncertain whether she could go through with it. "I kept telling myself, this is wrong," she'd later admit to investigators. It would be Maria Korp herself who sparked Tania into action. She walked into the garage on some or other errand and spotted Tania hiding there. For a split second, neither of the women moved. They stood eyeballing each other like predator and prey, each waiting for the other to do something, say something. Then Maria turned and tried to run, and Tania looped a garrote around her neck, the strap from a gym bag. The struggle was brief and one-sided. Within a couple of minutes, Maria collapsed to the floor, unconscious. Believing that she was dead, Tania then loaded Maria into the trunk of her car. The vehicle was driven into the Melbourne city center, where it was abandoned near the Shrine of Remembrance.

But Maria Korp wasn't dead. She would remain in the trunk for four days while police carried out an ever-expanding search for her. Eventually locating her car, the cops popped the trunk and found the missing woman, alive but only just. Maria was rushed to Alfred Hospital in a coma. She would remain in that condition over the next five months until doctors declared that she would never regain consciousness. The decision was then made by her court-appointed legal guardian to turn off her life support systems. She died on August 5, 2005.

So where did this leave Tania Herman and Joe Korp? The pair had actually been arrested and charged with attempted murder months earlier, on February 16, just days after Maria Korp was found. Herman had almost immediately confessed her part in the attack, naming Joe Korp as her co-conspirator. She'd subsequently entered a guilty plea at trial and had been sentenced to twelve years in prison, with parole eligibility in nine years. Korp, meanwhile, denied that he had played any part in Maria's death. He was awaiting trial for attempted murder at the time his wife died, with Tania due to testify against him. Now state prosecutors decided to up the ante and issue a warrant for murder. Before they could serve it, Joe Korp would be dead, swinging from a rope in his garage.

Oddly enough, the state declined to bring murder charges against Tania Herman. She served out her time and was released on parole in February 2014, having spent eight years behind bars. Tania had started a relationship with a fellow inmate named Nicole Muscatin in prison and Nicole was there to collect her on the day she walked free. After Joe Kolb, it appears she'd had her fill of men.

Three Times a Charm

Clay and Chanin Starbuck should have figured it out the first time around – a marriage between the two of them was never going to work. The couple had originally tied the knot in 1990 and had remained married for ten years, producing five children along the way. But the union was troubled from the start and, eventually, it broke down. In March 2000, they divorced. Then, to the surprise of friends and family, they announced just four months later that they were getting back together. That set up a tumultuous five-year period during which Clay worked on the Alaskan pipelines and Chanin stayed home and raised their kids. During this time, Clay frequently accused his wife of sleeping around and even claimed that their youngest child wasn't his.

Whether or not there was any truth to this accusation is a moot point. In any case, it did not deter Clay from asking Chanin to marry him for a second time. The couple exchanged vows before a magistrate in 2006. Four years later, they were back in court, dissolving their union yet again. Chanin got the kids. Clay got maintenance payments and a restraining order. She took out a lease on a house in Deer Park, Washington, close to her younger children's school. He rented a property about a half-mile away.

Walking away from a long-term marriage is never an easy thing to do, especially when there are kids involved. Relations between Clay and Chanin were tetchy at best, characterized by sniping and squabbles over arrear alimony payments. Angry texts were exchanged and Chanin even began keeping a journal, detailing her issues with her former husband. One of her complaints was that, despite the divorce, Clay still seemed obsessed with her sex life. At 42, Chanin Starbuck was still a very attractive woman. She had needs and chose to satisfy them with men who she met online, through various hookup sites. That did not sit well with Clay. He'd been obsessively jealous of Chanin while they were married and remained possessive of her, even after their separation.

But whatever Clay Starbuck's failings might have been as a husband, no one could fault him as a father. He was devoted to his children and insisted on picking them up each morning and driving them to school. On the morning of Thursday, December 1, 2011, though, Clay broke with routine. On this day, he sent a text to his former wife and informed her that she would have to take the kids to school, since his car had broken down on route. Chanin replied that she'd do so and dropped the kids off as arranged. She then returned to her residence. It was the last time that she'd be seen alive.

The first indication of something awry came at 2:45 that afternoon, when Chanin failed to collect her children from school, as was her habit. When one of the kids sent her a text, he got a response from Chanin saying that his father would collect him since she had a headache. The kids then waited a half-hour before trying to contact their dad. Unable to do so, they sent a text to an older brother, who picked them up and took them to their father's house. They remained there until evening and then went to a high school basketball game. One of the Starbuck children was on the team and Chanin was expected to attend the game but didn't show.

After the game, Clay took the children home but arrived to find the place locked and in darkness. The children would spend the night at his house. The following morning, an apparently concerned Clay Starbuck phoned the Spokane County Sheriff's Office and asked them to do a welfare check at his ex-wife's home. Officers responded later that day but found the house locked. They got no response when they knocked. Since they did not have a search warrant and since there was no obvious sign of foul play, they did not try to enter the property.

But on December 3rd, there was another call to the sheriff's department, this time made by one of Chanin's friends. Deputies were again dispatched to the house, entering with a key that they had obtained from the landlord. It was in the master bedroom that they found the missing woman. Chanin Starbuck was lying on her bed, her legs splayed, her naked dead flesh marred by numerous bruises and contusions. Whoever had killed her had taken his time posing the corpse, going for shock value and showing little respect for the dead. Chanin's legs were spread wide, and a dildo had been inserted into her vagina. A vibrator had been placed on her stomach with her hands folded over it. On the other side of the room, the door of a gun safe stood ajar. It contained, not firearms, but an extensive collection of sex toys. Whoever had murdered

Chanin Starbuck had been intent on one thing. He'd wanted to humiliate her. It immediately told investigators that this was personal, motivated by disgust and hatred.

As investigators continued processing the scene, the body was released to the morgue for autopsy. The coroner's report would fill in the gaps, describing the horrific details of Chanin's last moments. Burn marks on her chest suggested that she had been incapacitated with a taser. She had then been severely beaten, suffering head injuries and several broken ribs. Finally, she'd been strangled. Since there were no ligature marks, the coroner believed that she had been held in a chokehold, with her killer gradually cutting off her air supply. Chanin had not died quickly...or easily.

But who might have done such a thing? The obvious suspect was Clay Starbuck although Clay insisted that he was innocent. According to him, he'd been on his way to fetch his children that day when he had started having car trouble. His vehicle had stalled, and he'd been unable to restart it. He'd sent a text to Chanin, asking her to drop the kids off at school. Then he'd walked the short distance to his residence and gone back to bed. The first he realized that something might be wrong was when the children showed up at his house that afternoon. If the police really wanted to get to the bottom of this, he said, they should look into the many men that his ex-wife had been sleeping with, men she'd met on internet hookup sites.

This, of course, was a viable avenue of investigation and the police were able to track down Chanin Starbuck's current lovers. Not the "many men" that Clay had described but two individuals, one of them a married schoolteacher who had been using a false name to carry on his affair with the murdered woman. One of these men had a solid alibi. The other provided testimony which seemed to rule him out as a suspect. In any case, there was DNA evidence that seemed to absolve both men. A sample had been lifted from under Chanin Starbuck's fingernails. It did not match either of her lovers. It did, however, match her ex-husband.

With Clay Starbuck now firmly in the frame for his ex-wife's murder, the police began piecing together a likely sequence of events. They believed that Clay had faked the problem with his car to get Chanin out of the house. He'd used this opportunity to sneak in and hide, lying in wait until she returned. He'd then emerged from hiding and used a taser on her. Then, with Chanin writhing in agony on the floor, he'd begun beating and kicking her, breaking her ribs and fracturing her skull. Finally, he'd ended her life by throttling her to death. Then he'd taken his time inflicting a final humiliation on the woman who he felt had betrayed him. Investigators had always believed that this was a murder inspired by sexually motivated jealousy. Who but Clay harbored those feelings towards Chanin?

Clay Starbuck went on trial for the murder of his ex-wife in May 2013. He entered a not guilty plea, with his defense insisting that Chanin had been killed by one of her lovers. Unfortunately for them, this just didn't match the evidence. One of the men had attended a funeral that day and could thus be ruled out by alibi. The other had arranged a rendezvous with Chanin for 10:30 that morning but had arrived to find the house locked. He'd later tried calling Chanin and had returned to the house three times that day, looking for her. Why would he have done that if he knew she was dead?

The prosecution also introduced evidence regarding the odd usage of Chanin Starbuck's cell phone, on the day she was killed. At 9:18 a.m., there'd been a call to the Spokane County 911 line. No one was on the other end of the phone and when the dispatcher called back the call went straight to voicemail. Police believed that Chanin had tried to make this call while she was being attacked by that the phone had been taken away from her. Later that day, there were a series of peculiar texts, sent to both of Chanin's lovers. There was also the text to the children, telling them to wait at the school until their father collected them. All of these messages were sent after the coroner's estimated time of death. Prosecutors believed that they were sent by Clay Starbuck, to establish an alibi for himself.

And finally, there was that DNA, trapped under the victim's fingernails. Not even the defense could explain that one away. In the end, Clay Starbuck was found guilty of killing his ex-wife and sentenced to life in prison without parole. He continues to protest his innocence from behind bars. He retains the support of his children, who refuse to believe that he murdered their mother.

Desperate Measures

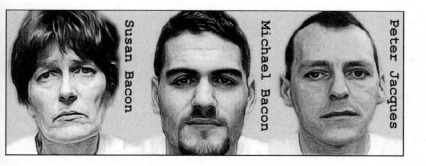

Susan Bacon

Michael Bacon

Peter Jacques

For most of his adult life, Nigel Bacon had dreamed of a job as a gamekeeper, managing the land and the wildlife on one of Nottinghamshire's grand estates. He'd all but given up on that dream when, in 2006, it came true. Nigel was appointed to oversee Clumber Park, a sprawling swathe of land covering idyllic parkland and dense forest in the East Midlands. Once, it had been the property of the Duke of Newcastle. Now it was a reserve for nature lovers and hunters. And it was all under the remit of Nigel Bacon.

But Nigel's dream job came with a complication. During the intervening years, he had set up a security firm, Keep It Security, which had gone on to be quite successful and had made him a moderately wealthy man, worth an estimated £350,000. Who would run the business while he was playing the role of country squire? The obvious candidates were his wife Susan and his middle son, Michael. But Nigel did not deem either of them competent or trustworthy and so he vacillated a long time on his decision. Eventually, though, he was left with no choice. Some of the responsibilities for the day-to-day running of the business were delegated to Susan and Michael. Nigel, though, kept a firm hand on the tiller.

So what was it that caused Nigel Bacon to regard his wife and son with such disdain? To find the answer, one has to understand the personalities of the people involved. This was no happy family. Nigel was a brutal man who ruled the household with an iron fist. He beat his wife frequently and with little provocation. He also was an abusive parent. In fact, oldest son Stuart had been removed from the family and placed in foster care after an incident that had landed both Nigel and Susan in prison. That happened in 1995, when a neighbor reported to police that he had seen both parents viciously attacking the boy. Charges of child abuse were brought, and convictions secured. Nigel would spend 18 months in prison, Susan 15 months.

The Bacons emerged from their respective periods of incarceration in 1997. But the time they had spent behind bars had done little to change their behavior. With Stuart no longer available to them, they turned their abuse on Michael, beating the boy, humiliating him, making his life a living hell. Nothing Michael could do was ever good enough for his father. Susan, meanwhile, used her teenaged son as a decoy. Whenever Nigel was in a bad mood, she'd direct his attention to Michael, usually with some concocted story of misbehavior. She'd do anything to save herself from a beating, even if it meant that her son suffered the consequences.

Given his tumultuous childhood, it should not be a surprise to anyone that Michael Bacon grew up to be a man beset by problems. He was particularly irresponsible when it came to money, racking up debts that he had no hope of servicing without the inheritance that he hoped to one day secure from his father. His hopes rested primarily on the family business, which his mother kept assuring him would soon be under his control. Susan had her own motivation for wanting this to happen. Michael might end up running the business, but she'd be the one pulling the strings. That would give her access to the company's cash flow, which would allow her to alleviate her situation. Like her son, Susan had massive debts. She also had a tax bill of nearly £40,000, which was due by November 2008. Without a sudden and substantial injection of cash, she'd be forced to declare bankruptcy.

And then Michael went and did something that derailed all of Susan's well-laid plans. He married a young woman who his father didn't approve of. Nigel's response was predictable. He disinherited his son and told him that he would never be given control of the family business. He also told Michael that he would no longer help with his debt situation, something he'd previously promised to do. This came as a crushing blow. Not just to Michael but to Susan, too.

One of the perks of Nigel Bacon's job at Clumber Park was that he was allowed to live at the historic Keeper's Cottage, a listed building on the outskirts of the park. This property had a long driveway with a gate at the end of it. During the day, the gate remained open. It was part of Nigel's routine to walk down and close it after nightfall. On the evening of November 26, 2008, Nigel was watching TV with his wife and youngest son, Tom, at Keeper's Cottage. During an ad break, he got up and headed out to close the gate, just as he did every evening.

But this evening would be different. Just a few minutes later, Nigel came staggering back into the cottage. His hand was clutched to his stomach, trying in vain to stem the blood that was welling between his fingers. There was blood spurting from a neck wound, too, and it was clear that he had also sustained a cut to his arm. "I'm hurt," he gasped before collapsing to the kitchen floor.

Susan Bacon did not even stop to check on the extent of her husband's injuries. The amount of blood alone told her that this was serious. She made a dash for the phone, picked it up, and dialed 999. "My husband went to shut the gate. He went through the door, and someone tried to stab him. There's blood everywhere!" she shrieked down the line. The dispatcher then heard her speaking directly to her husband. "It's alright. You're not going to die." In response, Nigel could be heard to say, "I love you."

When police and paramedics arrived a short while later, they found Susan Bacon standing outside, calmly smoking a cigarette. Nigel was still alive, but he'd lost a lot of blood and was unconscious. He was rushed to a local hospital but would die at 8:30 that night. Cause of death was attributed to excessive blood loss, exacerbated by the victim's heart condition. An autopsy would later determine that he'd been stabbed five times in the stomach, neck, and chest. There was also a wound to his left arm, presumably sustained as he tried to ward off his attacker.

The initial theory, promoted heavily by Susan, was that Nigel had encountered a would-be burglar on his way to the gate. If that was the case, then the attacker had been careless. Police found a black beanie and a black glove on the path. These would be submitted for DNA testing and would ultimately give detectives the identity of their prime suspect. Before that could happen, the police would find other clues, evidence that would implicate the not-so-grieving widow, Susan Bacon.

The first indication of Susan's possible involvement was when police found a note, in her handwriting, listing the key points of her story regarding a botched burglary. They also found a plan for an escape to Tunisia and details of that country's extradition protocols with the UK. Asked about these items, Susan attempted to deflect attention by suggesting that the police question her estranged son Stuart. According to her, Stuart "hated his father enough to do something like this."

However, it wasn't Stuart Bacon that investigators were interested in. It was his younger brother, Michael. Interviewed by detectives, Michael soon talked himself into trouble when he said that he'd been at his home in Mansfield Woodhouse, 11 miles away, at the time of the murder. A pingback from a cellphone mast proved this to be a lie. Michael had been within a few miles of the cottage at the time his father was killed. Did that mean that it was he who'd wielded the knife? The police didn't think so. They believed that Nigel Bacon had been killed by a hired assassin.

That idea was given even more credence when three different men came forward and said that they had been approached by Susan Bacon with offers of cash in exchange for killing her husband. Susan had apparently told these men that she was a victim of domestic violence but could not leave for fear that her husband would track her down and kill her. Unfortunately for Susan, the "damsel in distress" act hadn't worked. All three of the men had turned her down.

But Susan had found someone to do her bidding. Thanks to the wonders of DNA technology, the police now knew who that someone was. He was 29-year-old Peter Jacques, and he had plenty of motive to get involved in the murder-for-hire scheme. At the time of the murder, Jacques was even deeper in the hole than Susan and Michael Bacon. He owed more than £120,000 to various creditors.

Susan Bacon, Michael Bacon, and Peter Jacques were brought to trial at Nottingham Crown Court in November 2009. They entered not guilty pleas but there was plenty of evidence against them and plenty more that would emerge at trial. Cellphone records indicated that dozens of calls had passed between the three conspirators in the run-up to the murder. Detectives also learned that Peter Jacques had visited Clumber Park and had met Susan Bacon in the car park. At that time, she'd paid him a deposit of £1,000. He'd used part of it to buy a pair of black gloves, a black Adidas beanie, and a large kitchen knife from a Tesco supermarket in Mansfield.

Another piece of evidence to come out at the trial finally cemented Susan Bacon's role in the murder and showed just what a cold-hearted individual she was. At around the time that Nigel Bacon was knifed to death, the security system had been turned off at Keeper's Cottage. This would have allowed Susan to kill the outside lights and there could be only one reason why she'd want to do that. In the pitch dark of a country night, Nigel would not have seen his killer coming. He never stood a chance.

Modern jury trials often involve deliberations that go on for days or even weeks. In this case, it took the jurors just two hours before they returned with a guilty verdict against all three defendants. The sentence of the court was life in prison with a minimum tariff of 28 years for Jacques, 24 years for Susan Bacon, and 21 years for her son, Michael. The debt-ridden killers had entered into their deadly scheme to free themselves from crushing financial liabilities. And, in a way, their desperate measures had succeeded. Their creditors can't touch them in prison.

In the Dead of Night

Andrew Pixley

Some people are just born with strikes against their name and Armando Benavides was certainly one of them. Armando entered this world in Las Cruces, New Mexico on January 29, 1943. He was abandoned by his mother at age two, when she walked out on the family. Thereafter, he remained in the care of his father for two more years until the older man died of tuberculosis in 1947. That left the boy and his sister without familial support, and they ended up as wards of the state, shifted from foster home to foster home over the next decade. Then, in 1956, there was finally some good news. The children's mother had apparently seen the error of her ways. She'd settled down and married a man named Columbus Pixley, of Dallas, Oregon. She was finally in a position to care for her children. The now 13-year-old Armando found himself in a stable family home for the first time in his life. He even had a new name. He now went by Andrew Pixley.

But life with Andrew was no picnic, as his family was soon to discover. The boy was troubled, deeply so. Nervous and fidgety, the slightly built Pixley rebuffed all efforts of those who tried to get close to him. He made few friends and school and eventually dropped out without graduating. By then, he'd already built up a sizeable police file which included arrests for larceny and car theft. He'd later expand his repertoire to include fraud. Facing jail time for passing bad checks, he opted instead to enlist in the US Army. That, as you might expect, was not a good match. Within two years, Pixley had been discharged and was a civilian again, supporting himself by petty crime and menial jobs, drifting from place to place. That was how he end up in the town of Jackson, Wyoming in August of 1964.

Pixley had found a job there, working as a dishwasher at the Wort Motor Hotel and living onsite, in a trailer he shared with two other men, David Starling and Orval Edwards. The three men often drank together after their shift and did so on the night of August 5, 1962. However, Starling and Edwards eventually cried off and went to bed while a brooding Pixley stayed up to finish the bottle. Then, at some point in the evening, he left the trailer and went outside. There were lights still on in the hotel. He walked towards them.

Also staying at the hotel at that time was the McAuliffe family. Judge Robert McAuliffe was on the bench of the Illinois Circuit Court, while his wife Betty took care of their three daughters, Debbie, 12, Cindy, 8, and Susan, who was the youngest at just six years of age. The family was on a driving vacation and had stopped at the hotel for the night. They'd rented adjoining rooms with an inter-leading door. After dining together that evening, they had returned to their rooms where Betty tucked the girls into bed. She and the judge had plans to attend a show in the hotel that night.

Debbie would be babysitting her younger sisters. After kissing their girls goodnight, the McAuliffes departed.

We don't know for certain whether Andrew Pixley specifically targeted the room occupied by the McAuliffe sisters. Given the evidence, and what we know of Pixley's character, it is more likely that he chose the room at random, looking for something to steal. It was probably the large pile of firewood stack outside that drew his attention. This provided easy access to a first-floor window. Climbing the log pile, Pixley removed a screen from the window and entered. He probably expected to find the room empty but, of course, it wasn't.

Some hours later, just after midnight, Judge McAuliffe and his wife returned, opened the door of their room, and turned on the light. They were immediately met by a bewildering sight – Andrew Pixley, lying shirtless on the floor, covered in blood, apparently in a state of inebriation. Judge McAuliffe acted quickly, pinning the intruder to the floor while he shouted for his wife to call hotel security. But Betty had more immediate concerns. She ran directly for the inter-leading door, threw it open, and entered. In the next moment, she started screaming.

The inside of the room was like something transposed directly from a horror movie. Twelve-year-old Debbie was dead, her face beaten to a bloody pulp that was barely recognizable as human. Her sister, Cindy, was lying on the bed, face contorted into a terrible grimace, her tongue protruding stiffly between her blackened lips. Angry bruises on her throat suggested that she had been strangled. Only the youngest girl, Susan, was alive, although she was severely traumatized. God only knew what she had lived through. The arrival of her parents had undoubtedly saved her life.

By now, the ruckus coming from the McAuliffe's room had attracted the attention of an off-duty police officer who was staying at the hotel. As he entered to help the judge subdue the suspected killer, the local Sherriff's department had already been alerted. Help was on its way. Pixley was eventually brought from the building in handcuffs, with officers having to force their way through an angry crowd that was calling for him to be lynched. "I didn't do it," he kept mouthing as he was led to the waiting police car.

Over the days that followed, further details of the double child murder would begin to leak out, details that were extremely harrowing to hear. It emerged that both of the victims had been sexually assaulted before they were killed. Debbie had been bludgeoned to death with a rock that the killer had carried with him to the scene. Even more shocking with the fact that the little girl's nose had been bitten off and could not be found. The only conclusion that the police could draw was that Pixley had swallowed it. They could only pray that the child was already dead, or at least unconscious, when Pixley committed this horrific act of cannibalism.

And what did Andrew Pixley have to say about this? He began by insisting that he hadn't done it, that his Native American heritage would preclude him from doing such a thing. Later, after agreeing to be injected with sodium pentothal (the so-called truth serum), he said that he could remember drinking earlier in the evening but had no recollection of entering the room or killing the girls. He would maintain this stance right into his trial.

Justice moved swiftly in those days. Within five months of the murders, Andrew Pixley found himself on trial for his life. With little doubt as to the facts of the case, much of the testimony centered on Pixley's state of mind. There were genuine concerns that he might walk on a technicality but Dr. William Karn, who had examined the killer for 30 days at the Wyoming State Hospital, told the court that Pixley was quite sane. He described Pixley as a man who "hates the human race, himself included." He went on to say that the accused killer was an incurable sociopath, "one of the sickest I have ever seen." The chances of rehabilitating him were "absolutely nil."

During his testimony, Karn would also reveal something that Pixley had shared with him during their sessions. "He could have killed the girls while they were asleep," the psychiatrist said. "But it meant a lot to him that they were awake and aware of what was being done to them." At this point, the children's father, the normally composed Judge Robert McAuliffe, lurched out of his seat and tried to attack Pixley. Only the intervention of the bailiffs prevented him from doing so.

Andrew Pixley was convicted on two counts of first-degree murder after a trial lasting just three days. He was sentenced to die in the Wyoming gas chamber, a punishment that he apparently found quite amusing. He laughed openly as the sentence was read. This, again, proved just too much for Robert McAuliffe, who jumped out of his seat and shouted, "Laugh some more, you animal!" The killer happily obliged him as he was led away in chains.

Pixley's stay on death row would amount to just eleven months, almost unthinkable by today's multi-decade standards. During that time, he continued to insist that he could remember nothing of the murders. He did concede, however, that, "If I did something like that, I deserve what I get." That deserved treatment was delivered on December 10, 1965, when Pixley was strapped into the gas chamber at Wyoming Frontier Prison, known colloquially as The Old Pen. Pixley took a deep breath just before the cyanide pellets were dropped and held it for an extraordinarily long time. It took him ten minutes to die. No one, in living memory, had remained alive so long in the chamber.

In the aftermath of the murders, Robert McAuliffe sued the Wort Motor Hotel for the cost of psychiatric counseling that his surviving daughter would have to undergo. He and his wife also suffered untold mental trauma. It would result, ultimately, in the breakdown of their marriage. Like many parents of murdered children, the burden of grief would rend them apart.

The terrible misdeeds of Andrew Pixley are remembered to this day at the Wyoming Frontier Prison. His ghost is said to haunt the now disused death chamber. Meanwhile, the Wort Hotel is also rumored to host some restless spirits, in this case, the ghosts of the two murdered girls.

Hate Street

Stephen Sorton   Adam Swellings   Jordan Cunliffe

When Garry Newlove met his future wife Helen in a Manchester nightclub in 1982, it was love at first sight. The couple started dating and four years later, in 1986, they married. Money was tight back then and the couple could not even afford a proper honeymoon. But they were both hard workers and steadily improved their financial position over the years. By 2004, Garry was working as a sales director and Helen had a high-paying job as a legal secretary. That allowed them to purchase a newly built four-bedroom home for their family, which now included three daughters, Zoe, Danielle, and Amy. The house was on a quiet residential street in the town of Warrington, halfway between Manchester and Liverpool in the northwest of England. The only blight on their quiet, suburban life was a concrete, pedestrian underpass at the end of the road. This had become a magnet for rowdy teenagers at the weekend.

At first, the Newloves and their neighbors tried to ignore these gatherings. But as the months passed, the behavior of these youths became steadily more unruly, more anti-social, more aggressive.

The area around the underpass became littered with beer cans, liquor bottles, and drug paraphernalia. The youths also took to vandalizing cars on the street and to urinating in front of people's houses. Anyone who dared complain would be met with a barrage of expletives and threats of violence. It got so that people were afraid to go out at night. Some families even moved away from the area.

Complaints about this anti-social behavior were, of course, lodged with the local constabulary. But the police were stretched for resources and seldom came out to confront the offenders. On the occasions that they did, the youths would simply disperse, only to reconvene after the police were gone. And they were getting increasingly brazen. When a police liaison officer organized a town hall style meeting where residents could voice their concerns, gangs of youths descended on the venue and started banging on the windows and shouting abuse. After that incident, Helen Newlove remarked to a neighbor that it would take a murder before the police did anything. Those words would turn out to be tragically prophetic.

Friday, August 10, 2007, was a hot summer's day in Warrington, perfect weather for the local troublemakers to convene at a park for a drinking binge. The de facto leader of this collective was a 19-year-old miscreant named Adam Swelling, known to his friends as Swellhead. Swellings was well known to the police, having already accumulated a sizeable rap sheet that included arrests for burglary and assault. That very morning, he'd been released on bail, after he was brought in for assaulting a police officer. Now at liberty again, Swellhead was celebrating with his friends, downing copious amounts of beer and cider.

By late afternoon, the gang was well in their cups and now ready for a bit of recreational violence. They began prowling the streets and alleyways looking for likely victims. Several teenagers were attacked that afternoon, one of them a disabled boy of 16, who was pushed to the ground and then kicked and punched. Eventually tired out by these exertions, the gang convened to a pub where they continued drinking into the evening.

Just a few blocks away from this public house, the Newlove family was settling in for the night. Eldest daughter Zoe wasn't home. She was working a shift at IKEA. But Danielle and Amy were there, along with their parents. Helen, who was feeling unwell, had gone to bed early. That left Garry and his daughters to settle down on the couch for an evening in front of the telly. Their favorite talent show was on, and they were looking forward to watching it. Thankfully, the street outside appeared quiet. Perhaps the usual collective of rowdy teens had found somewhere else to sow their brand of mayhem.

But the peace would not last. At around 10:40 p.m. came the sound of drunken voices from outside, then the tinkle of smashing glass. Looking out onto the street, Garry could pick out one of the thugs smashing the brake lights on a neighbor's car. Then he saw one of the gang stumble towards Helen's Renault Scenic and start kicking it. "What's going on out there?" Helen called from upstairs.

"I'm just going out to check," came her husband's reply.

Perhaps Garry Newlove should have known better; perhaps he should have gritted his teeth and let the hooligans do their worst. Helen's car was insured, after all. It could be repaired. But Garry had had enough of standing by and doing nothing. This was the fourth time in as many weeks that the car had been targeted and he was going to have his say. Stepping out barefooted, he approached the youths and demanded to know which one of them had damaged his wife's car. He was met by a barrage of expletives, by being shoved and goaded and spat at. Then one of them (later identified as Adam Swellings) threw a sucker-punch, catching Garry on the back of the head from behind. That was when all hell broke loose.

That blow landed by their leader served as a catalyst to the rest of the hooligan gang. They swarmed in, punching and kicking in a frenzy that was likened by one neighbor to a pack of rabid beasts. Garry was pummeled to the ground, kicked when he fell, stomped on. Instinctively, he pulled himself into a fetal position but that offered little protection from the onslaught. The bones of his fingers were splintered as he tried to protect himself. That left his head exposed to their flailing feet. Blow after meaty blow was landed, fourteen in all. One of the attackers lost a shoe in the melee, another left the imprint of his sneaker on Gary's face. Not even the frantic screams of Garry's daughters, Amy and Danielle, could penetrate their homicidal frenzy. In the midst of all this, Zoe arrived home from work with her boyfriend. They tried to intervene but were held back by the gang members.

And then, after just two minutes of savage fury, the attack was over. The gang dispersed, sprinting away into the night. They'd later reconvene at a local chip shop to order takeaways and boast about their crime. In the meantime, Garry Newlove lay in a bloody heap on the ground. His daughter, Amy, had already called 999. Police and paramedics were on the way, but they could not get there soon enough. While the desperate family waited, Danielle cradled her father in her arms; Zoe's boyfriend gave CPR; Helen and Zoe and Amy held each other and cried hysterically. Then the ambulance was there, and Garry was rushed to the ER at the nearest hospital. There, doctors determined that he had 40 separate injuries, many of them life-threatening. A distraught Helen would soon learn that her husband was in a coma. By the following day, she would be told that he was braindead, with no possible chance of recovery. On August 12, two days after the attack, the horrible decision was taken to turn off life support. Gary Newlove, devoted husband, loving father-of-three, cancer survivor, was dead.

The Cheshire Police, who had been so passive in dealing with the problem of out-of-control youths, now went into overdrive hunting down the perpetrators. The first to be arrested was 16-year-old Stephen Sorton. Sorton swore that he had not participated in the attack, but he had lost his sneaker during the onslaught and had left it behind at the scene. Then followed nine more arrests in quick succession, all of them based on identification by eyewitnesses to the attack. Three names, however, were repeated over and over again – Stephen Sorton, 16-year-old Jordan Cunliffe, and 19-year-old Adam Swellings, the reputed leader of the gang. Swellings had admitted his participation in the attack to his mother and she had reported it to the police. Cunliffe, meanwhile, claimed that he had not gone out that night and was backed up by a family member. Blood found on his clothing made a liar of both of them.

By the time the matter came to trial on November 14, 2007, five youths stood in the dock at Chester Crown Court. This same venue had once heard testimony against Ian Brady and Myra Hindley, the reviled Moors Murderers. The five young men now charged with murder attracted similar revulsion. Their behavior during the trial would do nothing to improve their public image. Much of their time was spent joking and giggling, even as evidence of the horrific attack was heard, even as Garry Newlove's daughters recounted the trauma of seeing their beloved father beaten to death before their eyes.

But the accused were in a far less jovial mood once judgment was handed down. Two of the youths were acquitted but for Swellings, Sorton, and Cunliffe, it was life in prison, with minimum tariffs of 17, 15, and 12 years respectively. Swellings and Sorton responded to their sentences with stunned silence. Cunliffe, who had been the joker-in-chief during the trial, burst out crying and had to be comforted by his mother.

The aftermath of the Newlove trial would see intense public discussion on an issue that was plaguing the country at that time. This was not the first high-profile case in which out-of-control, drug-and-alcohol-fueled youths had turned homicidal. From pubs and workplaces to the tabloid newspapers, to parliament, the issue became a matter of national concern. The term 'Broken Britain' entered the common parlance. Something clearly had to be done.

And no one was more motivated to take action than Helen Newlove. In the wake of the tragedy, the grieving widow formed the Newlove Warrington foundation and threw her energy into multiple initiatives. These included campaigns to clamp down on the sale of alcohol to minors, to establish better support systems for victims of crime, and to ensure stiffer sentences for offenders. In recognition of her work, Helen was awarded a peerage in 2010. As Baroness Newlove, she currently holds the role of Victims' Commissioner, responsible for liaising with ministers on aspects of the Criminal Justice System that affect victims and witnesses.

Helen Newlove had once suggested to a neighbor that someone would have to be killed before the police took meaningful action against the prevailing yob culture. She could not have imagined that someone would be her beloved husband, Garry. On a warm August evening in 2007, Garry Newlove stood up against a gang of thugs who were vandalizing his family's property. It was his right to do so, perhaps even his obligation. He did not deserve to die for doing the right thing.

Do Unto Others

It is difficult to feel sympathy for a convicted murderer, especially one who has committed a crime so atrocious that a supreme court judge called it "butchery and barbarism." But it is possible, intuitive even, to take pity on the child who would become that killer. Often, these criminals emerge from childhoods fraught with deprivation, neglect, and abuse. Such was certainly the case with Janice Buttrum.

Janice was born in Adairsville, Georgia in 1963, to an unmarried mother who had no interest in raising her, no interest even in filling out the paperwork that would have put the baby up for adoption. Instead, she handed her infant daughter over to a dirt-poor, middle-aged couple, the Adcocks, who she barely knew. Janice would be raised in a ramshackle three-bedroom house without indoor plumbing or heating. Later, her "adoptive parents" moved to a one-bedroom trailer. Since there was no room for Janice there, she was forced to live in a broken-down van in the yard. The property was filthy, the floor littered with garbage, beer bottles, and moldering, half-eaten takeaway meals. Janice's diet consisted solely of junk food; her clothes were mostly scavenged from the local dump. Most of the money that her parents earned went on booze and they were violent drunks. The little girl was frequently beaten, told she was worthless, denied even a modicum of human kindness.

But as bad as that was, there was worse to come for Janice once she started school. She would arrive filthy, her hair matted, reeking to high heaven in her tattered, cast-off clothes. This, of course, made her an object of ridicule and disgust to her peers. Ostracized from the group, taunted and bullied, she existed on the fringes, friendless and lonely. Many kids lash out when placed in these situations, but Janice wasn't the violent type. She never retaliated against the playground taunts. Instead, she became increasingly introverted, a loner who seldom spoke unless spoken to.

Eventually, in her early teens, Janice decided that she had taken enough abuse from the Adcocks and ran away from home. This, however, would prove to be a case of "out of the frying pan, into the fire." She was befriended by an older man who offered her a place to sleep and then sexually assaulted her. He also handed her off to one of his friends. She was just 14 years old at the time. After that, she tried to return home, but the Adcocks no longer wanted her. They turned her over to the state authorities who placed her in a Youth Detention Center. Janice had committed no offense, but the state simply had no other place to put her. She would remain incarcerated for six months.

Shortly after her release from detention, Janice looked up her biological mother. The older woman still had little interest in her daughter, but she did introduce her to someone who would play a significant role in her life. Danny Buttrum was 26 years old, divorced, and the father of two children. He was also a drug user, a habitual drunk, and mentally impaired, with an IQ that bordered on retardation. He was no one's idea of a catch but Janice was infatuated with him. On the day that they met, he asked her to marry him and Janice said yes. Within a month, the 15-year-old Janice was a married woman.

Janice Buttrum had made many mistakes in her short life and this was yet another of them. Danny was an extremely violent man who became even more aggressive when he'd been drinking. And since Danny was drunk just about every day of his life, Janice had to endure frequent beatings, even while she was pregnant with the couple's first child. The police were constantly called to break up fights at their home. Janice also walked out numerous times, but she always returned. Again, this was out of desperation. She had nowhere else to go. Her only respite came in August 1980, when Danny received a short prison term for assault.

But Danny had no intention of serving his time, no matter how short it was. He'd barely begun his sentence when he escaped from the work farm, packed up his wife and infant daughter, and fled to Dalton, Georgia, some 30 miles away. There, Danny found work as a truck driver and the couple took up residence at a cheap motel called the Country Boy Inn.

Also living at the motel at that time was an attractive young woman named Demetra Faye Parker. Demetra was 19 years old and freshly arrived from Kenton, Tennessee. She had moved to Georgia to be close to her boyfriend and was staying at the motel while she sorted out more permanent accommodation. Although she kept mostly to herself, she took a shine to the Buttrum's 19-month-old daughter Marlena. When Janice asked if she'd babysit the child, Demetra readily agreed, waving away any suggestion of payment. Thereafter, this became a regular arrangement, even though Demetra confided in friends that Danny "creeped her out" and that she was wary of Janice. Those instincts would prove to be well-founded.

On the morning of September 3, 1980, the Dalton Police Department received a frantic call from the owner of the Country Boy Inn. One of the guests had been found dead in her room, her body so horribly mutilated that the owner could not find the words to adequately describe it. Police officers rushed to the motel and walked in on a scene that was every did as gruesome as the manager had suggested. Demetra Parker looked as though she had been mauled by wild beasts. She had been stabbed so many times that there was barely an inch of skin that had not been torn. In addition, an attempt had been made to slash her throat and the killer had also ripped the knife across her belly, slicing through the flesh and exposing the intestines. There was also evidence that the young woman had been raped.

Identifying a suspect for this heinous crime was easy. The motel owner told police that Demetra Parker had been friendly with two other guests, Danny and Janice Buttrum, and had sometimes looked after their baby daughter. Coincidentally, the Buttrums had checked out that very morning and had been seen driving away in Ms. Parker's car. A quick check on the background of the couple revealed that Danny Buttrum had a long police record and that there was currently a warrant out for his arrest, for escaping from a work farm in nearby Adairsville. Armed with this information, the police put out an APB on the Buttrums and on the stolen vehicle they were driving.

While this was ongoing, the body of Demetra Faye Parker was transported to Hamilton Memorial Hospital, for autopsy. Here the full, horrific details of the murder would be revealed. The young woman had been stabbed 97 times, all of the wounds inflicted with a short-bladed instrument, possibly a penknife. Sixty-seven stab wounds were counted to the chest, mainly concentrated on the left side. None of these penetrated deeper than two inches but the blade had nonetheless nicked several ribs and punctured a lung. Additionally, there were 24 knife wounds to the neck, including several slashes across the windpipe. Lacerations were also inflicted on the spine, cutting into the backbone. Then there were cuts to the genital area and the most grisly injury of all, a gaping wound to the abdomen which exposed the intestines. Forcible penetration had damaged both the vagina and the rectum and there were additional bruises to the scalp, nose, and knees, as well as a bite mark on her neck. As a final indignity, a plastic toothbrush holder had been forced into the victim's vagina. According to the pathologist, all of the injuries had been inflicted while Demetra Parker was still alive.

This was an unbelievably savage murder, one that the authorities were determined to resolve as quickly as possible. Someone capable of this level of savagery was very likely to kill again. Their fear was that the Buttrums might have fled the county by now, or even the state. It was also likely that they had ditched their stolen vehicle, which would make them more difficult to catch.

Fortunately for the police, the Buttrums were not very bright. The couple were still using their victim's car and had driven it to Pensacola, Florida. From there, Danny Buttrum contacted his mother, asking her to wire him some money. She agreed to do so but then passed the information on to the police. When Buttrum arrived to collect the cash, FBI agents were waiting for him and took him and his wife into custody. With extradition waived, the couple was soon on a transport back to Dalton.

Questioned by agents of the Georgia Bureau of Investigation, Janice Buttrum made no attempt to deny her part in the savage crime. According to Janice, she and her husband had gone to Demetra Parker's door at around 4 a.m. on the morning of the murder. Their intention was only to frighten the young woman, but things quickly got out of hand after Demetra tried to close the door on them. That angered Danny so he forced his way in and started struggling with Demetra, forcing her to the floor. Then he started stabbing her with his penknife, inflicting several wounds before handing the knife to Janice, who took up the attack. The couple continued in this way, passing the knife back and forth between them as they slashed and stabbed their victim to death.

That confession, of course, left out one very important detail. Demetra Parker had been raped and sodomized. Janice Buttrum initially denied any knowledge of the rape but later changed her story. Now she said that she had walked into Demetra's room and found her husband about to have sex with the young woman. That had sent her into a jealous rage, and she had attacked Demetra, stabbing her with the knife. She'd then urged her husband to rape the young woman. "I forced him into it," she said. "This is all on me."

Janice would maintain this story until just before the trial, when she described yet another version of events. After learning that her husband had informed the police that she had participated in the rape, including performing forced cunnilingus on the victim, Janice swung it around on him. She now insisted that it had been Danny's idea all along. She admitted stabbing Janice but said that she had only done so because she was afraid of her husband. This story, like the others, may have contained a kernel of truth but did not match the evidence.

The police had been able to construct their own hypothesis, based on the evidence of other witnesses. Friends of Demetra revealed that she was terrified of Danny, which seems to discount Janice's story that she had been prepared to have consensual sex with him. There was also the testimony of another hotel guest who said that he had been out cruising with Danny and Janice on the night of the murder. During the evening, Danny had consumed three six-packs of beer. He was very drunk but determined to pick up a young woman for sex. With his wife sitting in the backseat, he'd tried to proposition several women they passed on the street. Each of these women had turned down his crude advances. Eventually, frustrated with his lack of success, Danny had asked the man to drive him and Janice back to the motel. The man had then retired to his room and passed out.

But what of Danny and Janice? The police believed that the couple was still determined to find a sex partner for the night and had decided to rape Demetra Parker. Returning to their room, they'd woken Marlena and brought her to Demetra's room. They had then feigned some crisis with the child to get inside. Janice would later admit that her infant daughter had been present during the murder, crawling around on the floor and playing with the telephone while her parents butchered her babysitter.

Whatever had happened in that motel room on that dreadful night, two things were certain. A young woman's life had been brutally snuffed out and the perpetrators were in custody. Nobody expected them to receive much sympathy from a Georgia jury and those expectations turned out to be correct. Tried separately, they were both found guilty and sentenced to death. Janice Buttrum, who had been just 17 on the night of the murder, was going to the electric chair.

But neither Danny nor Janice would keep their dates with the executioner. Danny committed suicide by hanging himself in his cell at Whitfield County Jail in September 1981, a week after he was sentenced to death. Janice's sentence was later reduced on appeal to life without parole. Now in her late 50s, she remains behind bars. That is a good thing. Psychiatrists have warned that Janice Buttrum is a sexual sadist who is very likely to re-offend, given the chance.

For more True Crime books by Robert Keller

please visit:

http://bit.ly/kellerbooks

Printed in Great Britain
by Amazon

16830614R00088